Academic Workplace:
New Demands, Heightened Tensions

by Ann E. Austin and Zelda F. Gamson

ASHE-ERIC Higher Education Research Report No. 10, 1983

INDEX ISSUE, 1983 SERIES

Prepared by

 *Clearinghouse on Higher Education
The George Washington University*

Published by

Association for the Study of Higher Education

*Jonathan D. Fife,
Series Editor*

Cite as:
Austin, Ann E., and Gamson, Zelda F. *Academic Workplace: New Demands, Heightened Tensions*. ASHE-ERIC Higher Education Research Report No. 10. Washington, D.C.: Association for the Study of Higher Education, 1983.

The ERIC Clearinghouse on Higher Education invites individuals to submit proposals for writing monographs for the Higher Education Research Report series. Proposals must include:
1. A detailed manuscript proposal of not more than five pages.
2. A 75-word summary to be used by several review committees for the initial screening and rating of each proposal.
3. A vita.
4. A writing sample.

ISSN 0737-1292
ISBN 0-913317-09-8

 Clearinghouse on Higher Education
The George Washington University
One Dupont Circle, Suite 630
Washington, D.C. 20036

Association for the Study of Higher Education
One Dupont Circle, Suite 630
Washington, D.C. 20036

This publication was partially prepared with funding from the National Institute of Education, U.S. Department of Education, under contract no. 400-82-0011. The opinions expressed in this report do not necessarily reflect the positions or policies of NIE or the Department.

Richard Lonsdale
Professor of Educational Administration
New York University

Linda Kock Lorimer
Associate General Counsel
Yale University

Virginia B. Nordby
Director
Affirmative Action Programs
University of Michigan

Eugene Oliver
Director, University Office of School & College Relations
University of Illinois–Champaign

Harold Orlans
Lawyer

Marianne Phelps
Assistant Provost for Affirmative Action
The George Washington University

Gary K. Probst
Professor of Reading
Prince Georges Community College

Robert A. Scott
Director of Academic Affairs
State of Indiana Commission for Higher Education

Cliff Sjogren
Director of Admissions
University of Michigan

Al Smith
Assistant Director of the Institute of Higher Education &
    Professor of Instructional Leadership & Support
University of Florida

CONTENTS

FOREWORD

Higher education institutions have changed dramatically in the past 20 to 30 years as a workplace. Essentially, an institution is a workplace of two cultures: faculty and administrators. In the past, the faculty have been the dominant group affecting the conditions of the workplace with administrators being subservient to the influences of the faculty. Today the role and importance of each group has changed considerably and each affects the other as the institution adjusts to a rapid environmental and social evolution.

In this report, by Ann E. Austin, Assistant Professor in the Department of Education Administration and Higher Education, at Oklahoma State University and Zelda F. Gamson, Professor of Education in the Center for the Study of Higher Education and the Residential College at the University of Michigan, the literature on academe as a workplace, is carefully examined. Starting from a postion of reviewing the external pressures and the social structure of colleges and universities, the authors then examine the work experience of both faculty and administrators. From this review, the authors conclude with a series of policy implications and recommendations for future research agendas that will prove to be most helpful as institutional leaders strive to create a better balance between the needs of those working for the institution and the demands being placed in the institution.

Jonathan D. Fife
Director and Series Editor
ERIC Clearinghouse on Higher Education
The George Washington University

ACKNOWLEDGMENTS

We express our thanks to David Thomson of The University of Michigan for his attention to the typing of the manuscript. LaRue Cochran and Dorothy Risenbatt also were very helpful in preparing the manuscript. We are grateful to John Beck for his many bibliographic suggestions and continuing encouragement as the manuscript developed.

EXECUTIVE SUMMARY

For many years, the quality of worklife in universities and colleges has been seen as ideal compared to working conditions in other settings. But higher education is now experiencing pressures from several directions that may alter its assumed advantages for the people working in it. Under conditions of retrenchment, decisions are being made that may have momentous consequences for the quality of life of those who work in higher education and therefore for the quality and productivity of their institutions. More complete knowledge of the work experience of those employed in colleges and universities and greater attention to the quality of the university or college as a workplace could contribute to better performance.

How Do External Pressures Affect Universities and Colleges as Workplaces?

While the growth rate of revenues to colleges and universities has slowed, necessary expenditures have been increasing. With a simultaneous drop in enrollment at many institutions, economic pressures have led to salary cutbacks, the termination of positions, and fewer available resources. Shifts in the labor market have resulted in increased competition for available positions. Diminished public support has weakened the prestige of higher education, and increased federal and state regulations threaten institutional autonomy.

Universities and colleges are mixed organizations, operating basically with a bureaucratic structure on the administrative side and a collegial structure on the academic side (Baldridge 1971a, 1971b; Bess 1982; Corson 1960, 1975; Millett 1962). This duality has complicated decision making in colleges and universities for a long time. As current environmental pressures require the allocation of resources among competing groups, these internal structural tensions are heightened. In the face of rising costs, public demands for accountability, and a tight labor market, the collegial structure of colleges and universities is fragmenting. As more decision making occurs in the bureaucratic structure, power shifts away from the faculty toward the administration. This trend toward centralization changes the culture of colleges and universities, eroding the spirit of collegiality, the informal work style, and the support for autonomy characteristic of work within higher education.

Higher education is now experiencing pressures . . . that may alter its assumed [career] advantages. . . .

What Approach Can Be Taken to Examine Universities and Colleges as Workplaces?

The work experience of faculty, administrators, and support staff can be analyzed according to the characteristics of their work and work environment, the extent of their power and autonomy, and their relationship to the institution. Though variations in work experience undoubtedly relate to such variables as the type, size, and location of the institution and whether the institution is publicly or privately controlled, generalizations about institutions of diverse types are possible.

How Do Faculty Members Experience Their Work and Their Workplace?

Professors are professionals of a special type. In contrast to professionals in other areas, professors have different bodies of knowledge and responsibilities, which vary according to their disciplines. As members of both a profession and an organization, faculty members often face role conflicts and ambiguous demands concerning their research and teaching. Because a close relationship exists between the college or university where professors are employed and the nature of their academic work, external pressures on their institutions have considerable impact on the worklife of faculty members (Finkelstein 1978).

The role of faculty members is characterized by long hours and a variety of tasks (Shulman 1980). The particular allocations of faculty members' time to teaching, research, service, and publishing relate to the type of college or university where they work, their discipline, their age, and the stage of their career (Blackburn, Behymer, and Hall 1978; Ladd 1979; Pelz and Andrews 1976). The greatest sources of role strain for faculty are excessive demands to do too many discrete tasks (Baldwin and Blackburn 1981; Bess 1982; Finkelstein 1978). As financial pressures affect colleges and universities, professors carry heavier workloads and face conflicting demands. Restricted opportunity for growth is a major problem as well. Career paths in universities typically have short advancement ladders and flat salary curves (Kanter 1979). Many young scholars fail to find secure positions, and some tenured professors confront program cutbacks and in some cases the closure of programs and institutions.

Over the last decade, professors have lost 20 percent of their purchasing power (Anderson 1983). While this figure varies according to the type and geographic location of the institution and the faculty member's teaching area (Carnegie Council 1980), the conclusion cannot be refuted that extrinsic rewards for professorial work are declining. It is fortunate that such intrinsic aspects of their work as autonomy and freedom, intellectual exchange, and the opportunity to work with students relate most strongly to faculty members' satisfaction (Lewis and Becker 1979; McKeachie 1979). While intrinsic factors may be most important in promoting professors' satisfaction, however, extrinsic aspects of their work have been linked to dissatisfaction (Finkelstein 1978). If financial remuneration drops sufficiently low, faculty may express considerable dissatisfaction while still valuing the intrinsic motivators.

The research on faculty members' power and participation in organizational decisions indicates that professorial rank and credentials, institutional size, and institutional prestige relate to the degree of professors' power and autonomy (Baldridge et al. 1973; Cares and Blackburn 1978; Finkelstein 1978; Kenen and Kenen 1978). Current external pressures and the responses of colleges and universities to those pressures are threatening faculty autonomy (Carnegie Foundation 1982). Faculty members' participation in decision making also has declined over the last decade, especially in community colleges. These lower levels of faculty involvement in decision making and planning have been linked to declining morale among professors (Anderson 1983).

How Do Administrators Experience Colleges and Universities as Workplaces?

The experience of the senior administrator is changing as external pressures increase. Presidents feel considerable autonomy and power and report general satisfaction with their work. Increased state and federal regulations, however, often weaken the autonomy of campus officials (Kauffman 1980). While lack of time always has caused dissatisfaction, presidents are experiencing more stress as they deal with economic and other problems (Buxton, Pritchard, and Buxton 1976). Deans and department chairs are caught between the differing expectations of faculty and administrators (Booth 1982; Griffiths and McCarty 1980). As a result of greater budgetary problems and increasing demands for accountability, the strains of their positions multiply.

Middle administrators, the largest group of administrators, have a peculiar role in the mixed organizational structure of colleges and universities. While they implement policy, they seldom make policy decisions (Scott 1978). Despite limited opportunity for advancement, low status, and comparably low salary scales, the commitment of middle administrators to their institutions and to higher education remains high. Reasons for this commitment include the autonomy and freedom generally available in work in higher education, the opportunity to meet interesting people, and pride in the contributions higher education makes to society (Austin forthcoming; Thomas 1978). Their satisfaction remains quite high, too, though factors contributing to dissatisfaction include limited opportunities for advancement, limited time, and insufficient resources and staff (Scott 1978; Solomon and Tierney 1977). Given the frustrations middle administrators describe, it is surprising that their reported dissatisfaction is not greater. Perhaps the intrinsic rewards they enjoy serve as sufficient compensation. But if the extrinsic characteristics decline further, their commitment and satisfaction may be threatened.

What Conclusions and Policy Recommendations Emerge from the Study of Universities and Colleges as Workplaces?
Faculty and administrators traditionally have experienced varied, fairly autonomous work, good working conditions, and strong psychic rewards. Centralization of power and bureaucratization of decision making may be leading to a decline in morale, however. Administrators are not solely responsible for this shift. Rather, it reflects the limitations of the organizational structure of many colleges and universities as they have faced serious pressures from the outside. Competition both across and within departments means that the faculty as a corporate body cannot articulate their institutions' purposes or act together. This vacuum ensures the dominance of the bureaucratic structure. The shift also may mean that the traditionally "normative"

orientation of colleges and universities is becoming more "utilitarian."

The conventional response has been to push the structures and the people who work within them to the limits of their strengths. Such an approach will not succeed, except in the very short run. Instead, it is time that we enhance the limited efforts within higher education and the more extensive work in other sectors to improve organizational practice (Kanter 1983; Naisbitt 1982; Peters and Waterman 1982). We must take special care not to squander the strong commitment of many employees in colleges and universities. Leaders of colleges and universities must pay as much attention to the culture of their institutions as to their finances. They must learn how to articulate their institutions' purposes and to build structures for maintaining and increasing the commitment of all employee groups.

Task and decision-making structures must be more collaborative. Higher education could learn from the increasing attention industrial organizations are giving to management techniques that encourage participation (Powers and Powers 1983). Finally, programs for career planning and employee growth must become more pervasive. New ideas for expanding the mobility and choices of individuals in higher education include innovative arrangements of workload, internships in government or industry, short administrative assignments, and exchange programs (Schurr 1980; Toombs and Marlier 1981). We must use the best organizational research and practice so that the quality of worklife in universities and colleges can be improved. In the process, so will the quality of employees' performance.

What Are the Most Pressing Questions to Explore?
While a body of knowledge is developing about the academic institution as a workplace, further attention should be directed to the experiences of different employee groups in a variety of colleges and universities. Such institutional variables as size, selectivity, and public or private support should be considered. Much more is known about faculty and senior administrators than about other employee groups, particularly clerical staff, women, and part-time and minority employees. Comparative study with other

sectors—business settings, government, and service agencies—may provide useful ideas for colleges and universities dealing with retrenchment.

EXTERNAL PRESSURES AFFECTING THE UNIVERSITY AND COLLEGE AS A WORKPLACE

The growth of higher education in the several decades before the middle 1960s made universities and colleges desirable places to work, at least for faculty members and administrators. Steady financial support and high public esteem encouraged the feeling that higher education stood at the center of society. Faculty power was unparalleled, administrative opportunity wide open.

For the last 15 years, however, several external forces have combined to reduce the appeal of colleges and universities as work environments. Some of these forces have affected institutional structures and milieux directly; others have acted indirectly through their effects on the major actors—administrators, faculty, and staff—who most determine the nature of work in colleges and universities. These forces have deepened tensions that have been present in higher education for a long time.

[External] forces have deepened tensions that have been present in higher education for a long time.

First is economic pressure. The extent of financial support to higher education has been important historically in determining the atmosphere and activities of colleges and universities. The 1950s and 1960s, the "golden years," saw revenues for higher education increased dramatically. From 1949–50 to 1969–70, annual revenues in constant dollars expanded sixfold. Since 1969–70, the annual growth rate in revenues has leveled off to 5 percent or 6 percent; on a per-student basis, revenues have been increasing at a rate of only 1.5 percent since 1969–70 (Bowen 1978).

For three decades, the federal government devoted huge sums of money to financial aid for students, institutional programs, and research; that support has been shrinking—in some categories disappearing altogether. At the same time, state governments have restricted their support for higher education. The increase in state appropriations for 1982–83 was only 6 percent above appropriations for 1981–82. This situation is in marked contrast to the two previous decades, when state tax appropriations increased at an average of 14 percent per year (Magarrell 1982a).

At the same time, expenditures have been increasing. The impact of the U.S. (and world) economy is apparent in the widening gap between income and expenditures in many institutions. While the rate of growth in educational and general expenditures per student dropped in the early 1970s, the number of schools reporting expenditures exceeding income has been rising since the mid-1970s (National Center for Education Statistics 1980). The causes include inflation, rapidly rising energy costs, a more tenured and therefore more expensive faculty, and federal programs and regulations that require new administrative staff. In this situation, the drop in enrollments that has already hit some institutions and is projected to hit others very soon means greater costs per student.

Institutions have responded to this cost-income squeeze by freezing salaries, by limiting new construction and physical maintenance, and by not filling vacant positions (Mortimer and Tierney 1979). All of these measures have affected the quality of worklife in colleges and universities. Economic stringency, expressed in decreasing levels of state and federal aid to higher education and increasing costs, is the most powerful external pressure for change in the university as a workplace. Its mildest impact is seen in fewer new pieces of equipment and careful monitoring of expenses. Its most severe impact translates into minimal salary increases, program closures, and permanent layoffs.

Closely connected to these economic pressures are shifts in the labor market. Universities and colleges are particularly susceptible to an "opportunity squeeze": "More people, including people not traditionally in the work force, want more jobs, with better opportunity for career growth, and more chance for participation in decisions and power over events, at a time when the economy is not automatically expanding—and in educational systems, is even declining" (Kanter 1981, p. 556). Fewer positions, either for new or veteran faculty, pit more people against one another for whatever jobs are available. The young scholars who do manage to find positions have little assurance that they will receive the tenure that will guarantee them continuing employment. Those who already have tenure discover that they may have traded mobility for security, because the tight job market limits the opportunities open to them in other academic institutions. Under severe economic stringency, some tenured faculty may even face losing their once-secure jobs.

Pessimists among us suggest that fully one-half of all tenured professors are, or soon will be, locked in, blocked, frustrated, stuck, trapped. In addition, we now know that tenure is no protection against irrational

termination. There are signs that every year during the
mid-80's over 5,000 tenured professors may find their
positions eliminated. As college closings multiply—as
many as 500 could close in the next decade—the faculty
members will not be able to count on any institutional
base for possible alternate positions. Even should these
predictions prove to be far too pessimistic, no one
doubts that we are moving into a period when many
tenured faculty will need to reevaluate their careers and
reassess their economic situation (Schurr 1980, p. 1).

The influence of declining enrollments on the financial
difficulties of many colleges and universities, especially
those that cannot count on attracting traditional students,
has already been noted. Enrollment shifts have other
effects as well, and declining enrollments lie behind a
number of problems. "Most of the troublesome, professional, organizational, collegial, and client-related problems faced by . . . college professors are related in one way
or another to the dilemma of attracting students while
maintaining high intellectual standards" (Parelius 1981,
p. 13). Once colleges and universities had to grow to meet
the high demand for their services; now they must find
ways to stimulate enough demand. Many find themselves
analyzing their "image," looking into "marketing techniques," and "packaging themselves" to appeal to new
"clienteles." Such changes undoubtedly make institutions
more responsive, but they also communicate new and
sometimes conflicting messages to their employees.
Intertwined with these economic and demographic
forces are cultural and political forces. While higher education was hailed in the 1950s and 1960s as the answer to
everyone's problems, in the more sober 1980s it has lost
much of its special role. As a result, the professional status
of those who work in colleges and universities has declined. To make matters worse, regulations tied to the
disbursement of monies from the federal government and
statewide master planning have limited institutions' capac-
ity to determine their own fates.

. . . The most serious problem encountered by higher
education is the cumulative *impact of government inter-*
vention. Taken by itself, any single action may not be

unbearably intrusive, but the combined impact of many
actions can nearly suffocate an institution (Carnegie
Foundation 1982, p. 65).

The Carnegie Foundation report condemns state and
federal demands for greater accountability as "intrusive."
Arguing that these external demands threaten institutional
self-governance, it states that "campus leaders, from
presidents on down, feel caught in a confusing bureaucratic
web that demands accountability but provides few incentives for responsible decision making" (1982, p. 67).

Because of certain structural tensions and because of
limited experience in dealing with contraction, colleges and
universities have been especially vulnerable to these external pressures. The effect has been the erosion of some of
the qualities—the spirit of collegiality, the informal work
style, the support for autonomy—that university employees, particularly the faculty, have enjoyed. This aspect of
the current period of decline is only beginning to be recognized in higher education, at the very time that much
attention is being given to the quality of worklife in other
sectors of the economy. The striking feature of the current
situation is that higher education, as it has been forced to
deal with severe pressures, may be moving in the opposite
direction—toward lower participation, more hierarchy, less
job security, and blocked opportunity.

THE SOCIAL STRUCTURE OF COLLEGES AND UNIVERSITIES

While in many respects universities and colleges are similar to other organizations as workplaces, certain factors make them unique. Universities and colleges have traditionally been viewed as comfortable, low-pressure, "good" places to work. The special goals, purposes, and values of universities and colleges contribute to their distinctiveness. So does the complexity of their organizational arrangements, in which bureaucratic and collegial structures operate simultaneously. A good deal has been written about the social structure of colleges and universities and the ways it influences governance. This chapter examines what makes universities and colleges unique as workplaces, taking into consideration the impact of current pressures.

The Unique Organizational Structure of Colleges and Universities

For years, researchers have debated about the organizational and governance models that best describe colleges and universities. The literature on governance in higher education is oriented more toward the university than other types of institutions; consequently, this section pertains more to the university than to the smaller college in its analysis of organizational and governance models. While some assert that the university has a bureaucratic, hierarchical structure, others contend that collegial relationships are more characteristic. "Loosely coupled" (Weick 1976), "anarchic" (Cohen and March 1974), and "political" (Baldridge 1971a, 1971b) have been used to describe the university environment.

A number of investigators have ascribed to a bureaucratic model based on Max Weber's description of the formal organization of bureaucracy. A bureaucracy is an organization designed to meet its particular goals in the most efficient way possible. To achieve this end, a hierarchical structure is established by which authority moves downward from a chief executive office through a specified chain of command. Within such a system, authority and "legal rationality" are the dominant modes of interchange rather than friendship or personal loyalty. Promotion is awarded on the basis of competence, and payment is made according to formal criteria.

Some assert that the university [is] bureaucratic . . . , others . . . collegial. . . .

Corson (1960, 1975) asserts that universities follow a bureaucratic model in which the academic organization makes academic decisions and the administrative organization makes administrative decisions. Fixed salary scales, academic ranks, the tenure system, and the separation of personal and organizational property are all taken as evidence of bureaucracy in higher education. The university is a corporate person by virtue of its state charter, it has a formal hierarchy with established (though sometimes blurry) channels of communication and authority, it has a formal structure of rules and regulations and of record keeping and requirements, and decisions and problems often lie within the domain of a particular office (Baldridge 1971a). Blau (1973) also sees bureaucratic elements in the university's administrative hierarchy, formal division of labor, and clerical apparatus.

The "collegial model" is a common alternative advanced to describe decision making and governance within the university (Millett 1962; Parsons and Platt 1968). Supporters of the collegial model point to an informal hierarchy and identify the source of power within the university as based on professional expertise rather than on official position. According to the collegial model, the university is best characterized as a system of informal communication among a community of scholars. These scholars are professional equals who work together to make decisions through group consensus (Mortimer and McConnell 1978). These community-derived decisions are then implemented by the administration. "Compliance in institutions committed to high standards of scholarship and investigation is the product of reciprocal relationships depending on collegial associations, on the sharing of information, and on discussions and persuasion" (McConnell and Mortimer 1971, p. 3).

Baldridge (1971a) finds the collegial model too sanitized. The reality has a good deal more conflict in it than the collegial model admits. While consensus may occur eventually about a decision, it comes at the end of considerable dissent and jockeying. Arguing that neither the bureaucratic nor the collegial model explains faculty strikes, student unrest, and external pressure, Baldridge (1971a, 1971b) offers an alternative, the "political model." According to this model, the university is a pluralistic organization comprised of many diverse interest groups whose goals are not necessarily in harmony with one another. Each group articulates its own interests and tries to exert pressure on those making decisions. The dynamics of decision making depend on which groups interact and claim interest in a given issue. Through the "dynamic political process" by which these groups use their power and influence, decisions and policies gradually emerge (Baldridge 1971a, 1971b). Conflict erupts when the customary patterns of behavior guiding groups and positions break down.

The coexistence of collegial and bureaucratic frameworks is anomalous: "Faculty govern themselves through peer control and collegial norm enforcement, while staff units commonly are structured bureaucratically and hierarchically. Within these groupings, then, faculty interact with others of presumably equal status, while staff members agree to a differentiated power status in their organizational settings" (Bess 1982, p. 120). The framework of a college or university has "distinct architectural features" (Corson 1979, p. 5). The staff and line employees are in a relationship that is the reverse of what is found in business or government; while "the staff experts, the teachers and researchers, carry out the organization's production function," the administrators retain line authority over support staff (Corson 1979, p. 5). Furthermore, academic employees work within a relatively flat organizational structure, with few levels separating them from top executives, in distinct contrast to most industrial settings.

Katz and Kahn (1978) apply their theory of five organizational subsystems to colleges and universities: The president, deans, and department chairs constitute the managerial subsystem; the faculty the production system; the clerical and maintenance staff the maintenance subsystem; the admissions and other student support staff the supportive subsystem; and the institutional research staff the adaptive subsystem. An individual employee's work within the university is formulated largely by the demands of the subsystem of which the job is a part.

With bureaucratic and professional authority structures existing simultaneously and with a myriad of subgroups and individuals oriented toward their own as well as the institution's goals, the university is inevitably laden with conflict. Even in normal circumstances, the conflicts between hierarchical and collegial expectations laid on top of the loosely defined relationships between various university and college units (Weick 1976) engender "inadequacies in interunit and interpersonal relations in colleges and universities that are greater than in most profit-making organizations" (Bess 1982, p. 92). It is not clear, however, what "normal circumstances" really are. Certainly in the present situation of scarce resources—a situation likely to be normal for the next decade at least—it is clear that many issues arising in colleges and universities have implications for the allocation of resources. The allocation of resources inevitably engenders politics. Under certain conditions, it also leads to the centralization of power.

The Culture of Higher Education

Another important way to understand universities and colleges as workplaces is based on their culture. The mythology of academic culture portrays universities and colleges as places in which administrators, professors, and staff members gain satisfaction from their contributions to the intellectual development of students and to the production of knowledge for society. Since the mid-19th century, novels about university life such as Loring's *Two College Friends* (1871), Flandrau's *Harvard Episodes* (1897), Barnes's *A Princetonian: A Story of Undergraduate Life at the College of New Jersey* (1901), and Cather's *The Professor's House* (1925) have supported this view.

The culture of an organization has been linked to the kind of compliance system that characterizes the relationship between subordinates and superordinates. Compliance is "a relationship consisting of the power employed by superiors to control subordinates and the orientation of the subordinates to this power" (Etzioni 1961, p. xv). Compliance structures differ in organizations; in general, organizations can be divided into three types—normative, utilitarian, and coercive—according to their compliance structures. Colleges and universities are predominantly normative, with strong utilitarian elements, especially on the administrative side (Etzioni 1961). Reward systems in colleges and universities are based primarily on the belief that a university is involved in good work. Given this kind of culture, faculty and administrators "attracted to institutions of higher education will likely include individuals possessing much intellectual curiosity . . . [who are] willing to trade greater rewards for a relatively free and unregimented work style" (Corson 1979, p. 4).

Responses to external pressures seem to be changing the appeal of universities and colleges. External demands for accountability, for example, have led to a greater emphasis on the measurement of outputs and formal evaluation. If faculty, administrators, or staff feel that employment policies made in response to external pressures do not reflect a recognition of the quality of their services and of their commitment, they may withdraw their normative attachment to their institutions and to higher education in general. They may come to perceive their work as more "utilitarian" than "normative" (Etzioni 1961).

Summary
Because the university or college is a unique workplace with both bureaucratic and collegial structures, it has built-in tensions. While some employees, such as department chairs and deans, live in both worlds, other employees, such as many mid-level administrators, faculty, and nonacademic clerical staff, are more clearly located in one or the other. At times, authority centered in a particular office in the bureaucratic structure may conflict with authority based in the collegial structure. The collegial structure itself has been shaped in recent years by the rapid growth of higher education after World War II and by an "academic revolution" that has weakened institutional (as opposed to disciplinary) loyalty (Jencks and Riesman 1968). The current pressures from the external environment heighten those tensions as resources must be allocated in new ways. The collegial structure has become so fractured in many institutions that it can do nothing more than provide the backdrop for departmental competition over scarce resources. One result is that decisions normally reserved for the collegial structure are made in the bureaucratic structure. This shift in power away from faculty toward administrators is probably the most important change that has occurred in higher education in recent years. It may move the culture of colleges and universities away from normative to more utilitarian values. And it is undoubtedly affecting the way academic workers experience their institutions and their work.

The life of a professor has been portrayed as quiet and somewhat sheltered, but whether that portrayal was ever true is uncertain. In any case, as financial pressures and institutional tensions make the life of the professor less secure, "the future looks different from what most professors expected when they got into teaching" (Larkin and Clagett 1981, p. 1). Research on the work experience of faculty is extensive, but it is fragmented and rather unorganized. This review identifies the most important characteristics of the work experience of faculty members and considers the impact of current environmental pressures on those characteristics, including the extrinsic and intrinsic elements of faculty members' work, their power and autonomy, their relationships to the institution, and the outcomes of their work.[1] Table I in the appendix summarizes findings concerning the work experience of faculty members.

Professionals with a Difference

Those who view college teaching as a typical profession cite the "basic body of abstract knowledge," the "ideal of service," the high social status, prestige, educational credentials, and autonomy, and the peer review of professorial work (Blau 1973). In some important respects, however, professors differ significantly from other professionals. While the work of the academy is based on a body of abstract knowledge, that body of knowledge differs for each discipline. The specific responsibilities of academic work and faculty orientations toward research and teaching also vary across disciplines (Finkelstein 1978). The service ideal of the professional generally requires serving the needs of clients through the exercise of detached, objective expertise. Yet professors are expected to be much more involved with their clients, especially graduate students, than are other professionals. Aside from students, the clients of faculty are diffusely defined and diverse—peers, the general public, and sometimes governmental or private funding agencies (Bess 1982; Blau 1973; Light 1974).

The professorial role also differs from other professions in acceptable career routes. While most professions offer

[1]Much of the literature discussed was first analyzed in Finkelstein's comprehensive review (1978). The particular challenges that part-time faculty face are not included in this review.

several possible legitimate career routes, in higher education only one is promoted as the ideal. A graduate of law school will be considered equally successful as a lawyer, judge, law professor, or executive. "In the scholarly professions, [however,] . . . new members are trained only to be scholars, even though only a fraction of them will publish" (Light 1974, p. 16). Furthermore, more than in other professions, it is the employing institution that defines the professor as a professional: "A doctor is a doctor wherever he may be, but a professor is a professor only if employed by a college or university. This close connection with one type of institution means that the structure of the institutions and the nature of academic work have always interacted with each other" (Light 1974, p. 17). For this reason, external pressures on colleges and universities can profoundly affect the worklife of faculty members.

Not only are universities and colleges different from other workplaces. The position of academic professionals within them also has peculiar dynamics. The simultaneous membership in a profession and an organization often leads to role conflicts (Baldridge 1971a, 1971b; Scott 1966; Stonewater 1977). For many faculty members, conflict often occurs between the organization's demands for productivity as evidenced by research and their preference for teaching. Believing that research is the most rewarded activity in their institutions, they are troubled if they are not engaged in it (Hind 1969; Ladd 1979). Professors' sense of what faculty should be doing is not in line with "what they actually do and want to do" (Ladd 1979, p. 5). Faculty members who see good teaching as a priority for higher education do not feel they receive encouragement for it from colleagues, especially at research universities (Blau 1973). Faculty often receive mixed signals about how to allocate their energies among research, teaching, and service to achieve tenure. Assistant professors in particular feel that criteria for review are ambiguous (Rich and Jolicoeur 1978). The strain is greatest when research-oriented faculty are pushed to teach and teaching-oriented faculty are pressured to do more research (Finkelstein 1978).

In addition to mixed signals about priorities, the faculty's daily responsibilities add to strain. "The central source of role conflict/strain lies in 'incongruous demands'

Faculty often receive mixed signals about how to allocate their energies among research, teaching, and service. . . .

placed upon faculty" (Finkelstein 1978, p. 309). Faculty are often pressured by excessive demands and too many discrete tasks (Barnard 1971; Bess 1982; Larkin and Clagett 1981; Parsons and Platt 1968). Teaching load increases role strain (Morgan 1970). The burden is apparently spread unevenly: In Morgan's study, natural scientists had the lowest teaching load and the least role conflict; humanities and social science faculty carried heavier teaching loads and experienced greater role strain.

The research on role conflict is plagued by several problems (Finkelstein 1978). The dependent variable, role conflict, is inconsistently defined across studies. Sometimes role conflict is indexed by incompatibilities between teaching and research, while in other studies it is defined as the strain created by conflicting demands from the various members of a professor's role set. Studies also differ in how they define the members of the professor's role set; usually students and administrators are treated inconsistently. Whatever the solution to these conceptual problems, however, it is clear that as colleges and universities offer tenure to fewer professors, how faculty should spend their time will become a matter of great import. Economic pressures that lead to cutbacks in clerical support, equipment, and positions will mean that the remaining faculty will have more work and therefore greater role strain.

Extrinsic Factors in Faculty Work
The sociological literature on work discusses both extrinsic and intrinsic dimensions of jobs. Extrinsic dimensions focus on the environment and conditions under which the work is done. They usually include workload, working conditions, supervisory practices, rewards, opportunity structures, and other policies regulating the conditions of employment. Intrinsic factors pertain more to the nature of the work itself—how it is done and how it affects the employee. Among intrinsic dimensions are the variety of different activities involved in doing the work, the degree to which the employee performs a task from beginning to end, the autonomy the individual has in doing the work, the responsibility involved, and the amount of feedback concerning performance that the employee receives. This section analyzes the extrinsic aspects of faculty work, focusing especially on workload and activities, opportunity

structure, and reward structure. The following section focuses on the intrinsic aspects of faculty work.

Activities and workload

In recent years, as universities and colleges have been pressured to cut costs, the study of faculty workload has received considerable attention. Increasingly, "higher education is recognized as a contracting industry experiencing the full impact of the problems of today's economic workplace. . . . These pressures . . . are compelling college managers to seek ways of reducing personnel costs, while at the same time striving to deliver a quality output within a labor-intense framework" (Douglas, Krause, and Winogora 1980, p. 1). The literature on faculty workload includes quantitative studies, such as analyses of credit hours taught, contact hours, and student full-time equivalent credit hours produced, as well as faculty members' reports of their own activities (Ladd 1979; Parsons and Platt 1968; Shulman 1980; Wendel 1977; Willie and Stecklein 1981; Yuker, 1974).

A common theme in studies of faculty workload is that professors are engaged in a wide variety of tasks. As already noted, excessive demands to perform discrete tasks are the greatest source of role strain for faculty members (Baldwin and Blackburn 1981; Barnard 1971; Bess 1982; Larkin and Clagett 1981; Morton 1965; Parsons and Platt 1968; Wendel 1977). While variety is important for meaningful, satisfying work in less skilled jobs (Hackman and Oldham 1980), too many different responsibilities may threaten those in highly skilled jobs.

> It would appear that college instructors are asked to do many different things and need to spend long hours to accomplish those tasks. If the concerned publics are interested in getting the most out of the professor, they may need to give serious consideration to the problem . . . that many professors work at a lower level of efficiency because they are doing too many things (Wendel 1977, p. 84).

As faculty and staff positions are cut, fewer professors will be required to handle more responsibilities, a requirement that will increase pressures on faculty members' time.

Faculty members report average work weeks of between 44 and 55 hours (Ladd 1979; Shulman 1980; Wendel 1977). Faculty activities have always been divided between teaching and scholarship, with service activities more an afterthought. Students of higher education have classified professors as academics with professional orientations or academics with organizational orientations (Lazarsfeld and Thielens 1958), as scholars or educators (Wilson 1964), or as cosmopolitans or locals (Gouldner 1957, 1958). Issues of classification aside, it is clear that the great majority of faculty members express a preference for teaching. When asked to identify themselves as "scholars"/"scientists"/ "intellectuals" or as "teachers"/"professionals," 70 percent of all faculty members chose the second group of categories (Ladd and Lipset 1975, 1977). Among respondents from two-year colleges, 93 percent chose the teacher role, while the figure for faculty in research universities was 50 percent (Ladd 1979).

In 1977, 47 percent of professors spent more than 10 hours teaching each week, 30 percent had 13 or more hours in the classroom, and only 17 percent spent four hours or less in class (Ladd 1979). The allocation of time is related to the type of institution, with faculty at elite institutions spending less time teaching than faculty at less prestigious institutions (Fulton and Trow 1974; Parsons and Platt 1968; Shulman 1980; Willie and Stecklein 1981; Wilson 1964). At two-year institutions, 70 percent of faculty time was devoted to teaching activities, while the comparable figure at four-year colleges was approximately 50 percent and at doctoral-granting institutions 33 percent (Shulman 1980). The median percentage of faculty members' time spent on such activities in 1980 at four-year institutions was 60 percent compared to 80 percent at community colleges (Willie and Stecklein 1981). A random sample of 75 faculty members at eight California institutions of different types found that 95 percent of junior college faculty spent 75 percent or more of their time on teaching activities compared to 30 percent of the faculty members at doctoral-granting universities (Rich and Jolicoeur 1978).

University faculty members, however, devote greater proportions of time to research than do faculty at other types of institutions. Less than one-quarter of a group of respondents had published extensively (defined as 20 or more articles or three or more monographs), and more than one-half had published "nothing or very little" (Ladd and Lipset 1977). Only 28 percent of the respondents from major research universities published "very little" or not at all, however, in contrast to 87 percent of the faculty from two-year colleges (Ladd 1979). Fifty-five percent of university faculty spent half or more of their time on research, while the comparable figure among junior college faculty studied was 3 percent (Rich and Jolicoeur 1978). Faculty in doctoral-granting institutions spent between 50 and 100 percent more time on research and graduate training than did faculty at other types of institutions (Baldridge et al. 1978).

At elite institutions, faculty members active in research were also likely to be involved in administration; those not active in research were less active in administration (Fulton and Trow 1974). Allocation of time for teaching did not vary according to research orientation in elite institutions. In contrast, at lower-quality institutions, professors who were not active researchers were more likely to take administrative roles. These less active researchers also spent more time teaching than their research-oriented colleagues. Perhaps the faculty role at high-quality institutions may be more "integrated," while at lower-quality institutions, research and teaching are more likely to be distinct, thus causing a more "fragmented" role for faculty (Fulton and Trow 1974).

While such comparisons of faculty members' activities have been made across institutional types, very little research has focused on differences in activities among disciplines. Rich and Jolicoeur (1978) did observe that faculty in education and the fine arts, which "focus on individual instruction, have the greatest preference for and the most time involved in teaching" (p. 440). While more than half of the faculty respondents in these areas preferred teaching over research, only 29 percent in the natural sciences and 38 percent in professional studies preferred teaching.

The age of the individual and stage in one's career appear to relate to the way faculty members allocate their time and to their productivity. Professors' interests shift from research to teaching with increasing age (Fulton and Trow 1974). Comparing professors aged 31 to 35 with those aged 56 to 60, Fulton and Trow found that the percentage who identified themselves as "exclusive teachers" doubled, while those who selected the term "strong researcher" declined by half. While orientation toward teaching may increase with age, the amount of time actually devoted to class preparation appears to decline as faculty members move up in rank (Thompson 1971). Productivity as measured by publication follows a saddle-shaped curve (Blackburn, Behymer, and Hall 1978; Pelz and Andrews 1976). While the young professor spends considerable time in research, this productivity drops as associate professorship is reached and rises again when full professorship is reached. The third component of faculty work, service, appears to increase over the years. Faculty members appear to get more involved in service activities as they become more comfortable with their teaching responsibilities and less pressured by demands for scholarship (Baldwin and Blackburn 1981).[2]

"Internalized standards of professional performance strongly affect faculty members' use of their time" (Finkelstein 1978, p. 246). Although four-fifths of the faculty at Stanford felt research was most important in the determination of rewards, they spent most of their time on teaching activities (Hind 1969). Similarly, perceptions of what was rewarded were independent of faculty members' allocation of their time and effort (Borland 1970). Borland concluded that faculty choose what they want to do, which then affects the institution's goals and workload assignments. Professors' "self-expectations" explained 30 to 40 percent of the variance in time allocation among teaching, research, and administrative work, while the organization's expectations, as reflected in the workload assignment, explained only 9 to 30 percent of the variance. Expectations of colleagues and chairs explained 0 percent to 3 percent (DeVries 1970).

The impact of the work assignment appears to vary with the degree of control faculty exercise (Finkelstein 1978). "In those cases where control over work load is high, self-expectations dominate; in those situations where it is lower, faculty activity patterns are more likely to be sub-

[2]McKeachie (1983) summarizes the research on the effects of aging on faculty members' productivity and offers ideas for enhancing the productivity of older faculty members.

ject to the independent effect of work load assignment"
(Finkelstein 1978, p. 246). New Ph.D.'s spent more time in
teaching and research than did more established faculty
members (Klapper 1967), which may be explained by the
fact that young professors have less control over their
work assignments (Finkelstein 1978). Most of these studies
(except Klapper's) have been conducted at research-
oriented institutions. While less systematic information
is available on time allocation and control at lower-
quality institutions, it is possible that the way such faculty
members spend their time is subject to greater institutional control than at higher-quality institutions (Finkelstein 1978).

Several recent comparative studies suggest that many
faculty, while they may continue to prefer teaching, feel an
increasing need to publish. Dedication to good teaching
continues, but professors at all institutional types indicate
more interest in doing research (Rich and Jolicoeur 1978).
Among the California junior college faculty studied, for
example, 44 percent reported that they had an interest in
research, though only 16 percent preferred research over
teaching. In another study, faculty reported spending less
time on research activities in 1980 compared to 1968, but
they published more (Willie and Stecklein 1981). A reasonable interpretation of this finding is that the tighter academic employment market, the steady state of enrollment,
and the decline of resources are forcing faculty members to
publish their work more regularly—and perhaps more
quickly—than they did in the past. The trend toward a
greater emphasis on publishing could have long-term
implications for colleges and universities:

> *It will be interesting to see whether the institutional
> milieu will socialize future academicians into the prevail-
> ing norms, thus maintaining the large traditional differ-
> ences between types of colleges, or whether the influx of
> research-oriented faculty, coupled with pressures from
> professional disciplines, will tend to lessen these differ-
> ences and thereby bring about the ascendancy of disci-
> pline-oriented cosmopolitan values over institution-
> oriented local values* (Rich and Jolicoeur 1978, p. 443).

Faculty workload is becoming a significant issue as
universities and colleges try to do more with less. The

development of allocating workload according to differences in discipline, institutional type, and teaching level is a pressing challenge.

> *In the 1980's, workload will develop a dual meaning in institutional terms. It will retain its meaning of how many hours faculty work and what that figure suggests in view of the institution's need for effectiveness and efficiency. In addition, workload will refer to working conditions for faculty in which the kind or quality of workload is linked to faculty and institutional renewal* (Shulman 1980, p. 11).

Opportunity structure

A concept that has been receiving attention in the sociological literature in recent years is the structure of opportunity within work organizations. Opportunity is a key variable that determines the nature of individuals' work experience. Workers can be divided into "the moving," those who expect to move to a higher level, and "the stuck," those who perceive only a short job ladder with little chance for mobility (Kanter 1977, 1979). Individuals who see themselves as "stuck" develop lower aspirations and feel lower self-esteem than "the moving." Feeling little attachment to their work, the stuck tend to disengage themselves, becoming "psychic," if not actual, dropouts. The stuck are likely to take few risks, look to peer groups or outside the organization for personal attachments to protect their self-esteem, and express dissatisfaction through griping and resistance to change.

The moving, in contrast, take satisfaction from their work and have high aspirations. They assess their skills and abilities highly and work hard because they see potential rewards for their efforts. The moving form political bonds with individuals higher in the organizational structure and identify with those who hold power. When they have a grievance, they are likely to express themselves directly.

Kanter's hypotheses relate degree of opportunity to the person's entire work experience. Career paths within the university have short advancement ladders, flat salary curves, and limited career paths (Kanter 1979). Growth within a job in higher education often comes through new responsibilities or a title change rather than a promotion. Higher education is characterized by a "pyramid squeeze" (Kanter 1979); that is, there are few jobs at the top to which employees can aspire. The difficult current economic situation also contributes to the tight job market and adds to the frustration of those wishing to move up. These various characteristics and factors suggest that faculty and staff may be prone to a sense of being "stuck." Within the academic community, the assumption continues that " 'a good man will take care of himself.' Meanwhile, the failure to provide significant mid-career opportunities, including avenues for beginning new careers, eats at the heart of the academic enterprise" (Kanter 1979, cited in Schurr 1980, p. 2).

The problem involves professors and scholars of several types: (1) secure faculty members who feel stuck; (2) tenured faculty whose programs are being terminated but who might be placed in other positions within the institution; (3) tenured faculty in institutions that are closing; and (4) scholars unable to secure a position in a university or college (Keyfitz 1975; Schurr 1980). With fewer academic positions available, "a displacement process occurs by which Ph.D.'s from the more highly reputed institutions take the jobs that in an earlier time would have gone to graduates of less illustrious schools, and the latter then have to drop down to undergraduate teaching, perhaps in junior colleges" (Keyfitz 1975, p. 8). This domino-like effect means that many scholars are holding faculty positions with responsibilities different from their preferences, while other scholars cannot secure positions at all.

Limited opportunity varies according to institutional type, regional economic situation, and faculty members' personal circumstances (Schurr 1980). Faculty at community colleges or at research universities are not affected by limited opportunity as much as those at the "second level state universities and colleges" and the "nonelitist private colleges," where faculty are pressured to do research while also carrying heavy teaching loads (Schurr 1980, p. 6).

The reasons many tenured faculty in this . . . group of institutions feel stuck is that they do not perceive their careers to be open-ended. They find themselves confined to a fixed "track" in a closed educational system. Fac-

Growth . . . often comes through new responsibilities or a title change rather than a promotion.

ulty members who have been trained to think individually, even in isolation, have this self-definition reinforced by institutional policies which define faculty obligations in terms of specialized competencies and assigned courses (Schurr 1980, p. 67).

Limited opportunity is especially severe for faculty at geographically isolated institutions and at institutions located in areas of economic depression. In those situations, available nonacademic jobs may be few. Faculty members at institutions experiencing financial difficulties are also among those most likely to face this problem. In relationships involving two people with careers, professors often face additional, usually painful, choices involving not only themselves.

"Expanding career horizons for professors is probably inseparable from revitalizing their educational environments" (Schurr 1980, p. 8). Only a few programs deal with the problem directly. The best program, in Schurr's opinion, is Loyola University's "Career Development Program," underwritten by the Fund for the Improvement of Postsecondary Education. This program addresses the needs of professors who are institutionally "stuck" by providing workshops, internships, and counseling. While some New England and Great Lakes area universities offer programs to deal with the problem, the national picture reflects little planning or innovation. An important aspect of the problem could be approached indirectly, as Schurr suggests, by paying greater attention to the effects of changes in educational environments on the faculty. Thus, for example, participation in new forms of teaching and research that make use of, but go beyond, disciplinary boundaries seems to be one important source of vitality for faculty (Gaff 1983; Gamson forthcoming). These efforts do not speak to the problems of terminated faculty members, who have been largely ignored. As it threatens the commitment to and vitality of the academic profession, the problem of restricted opportunity for faculty deserves special attention in institutions and national policy circles (Herman, McArt, and Belle 1983; Rice 1980).

Reward structure
Faculty members are bound to their institutions as much by intrinsic rewards—the nature of their work as teachers

and researchers and their interactions with colleagues and students—as by extrinsic rewards like salary and benefits (Lewis and Becker 1979). In fact, intrinsic factors may be most important in promoting faculty members' satisfaction. Nevertheless, the extrinsic factor of salary has been linked to dissatisfaction and, given recent trends, has become a significant problem for faculty members.

Compensation for faculty has dropped in comparison to cost-of-living increases over the last decade (Carnegie Council 1980). While the average faculty salary has increased 72.9 percent over the last decade and faculty members of all ranks at all types of institutions earned an average salary of $23,650 in 1980–81, average salaries would have been $29,345 if they had increased at the rate of the cost of living (Magarrell 1981). Faculty have lost 20 percent of their purchasing power in the last 10 years (Anderson 1983). It is also significant that faculty compensation has dropped compared to the average compensation for civilian employees (Carnegie Council 1980). When comparisons are made between professors, the decline in faculty salaries in recent years is very apparent. For example, while dentists and professors earned similar salaries in 1940, dentists earned 175 percent more than professors in 1980 (Anderson 1983).

Because the drop in salaries relates to declining and shifting enrollments (Carnegie Council 1980), "some faculty members will be more affected than others: those in the East and North, in comprehensive colleges, in less selective four-year liberal-arts colleges, in doctorate-granting universities, in the humanities, in nontenured ranks, and in closing and merging institutions" (Bucher 1981, p. 22). Compensation varies according to institutional type, with faculty at doctoral-granting universities earning, on the average, the highest salaries. In 1980–81, the average salary for faculty at all ranks at private doctoral-granting universities was $27,930, compared to $24,290 at private, nonchurch-related institutions, $24,150 at public institutions, $19,450 at church-related institutions, and $14,440 at church-related junior colleges (Magarrell 1981). The average salary for faculty members at all levels in two- and four-year universities and colleges for 1982–83 was $27,430. The average faculty salary at universities was $31,010, compared to $23,700 at two-year colleges and

$22,890 at undergraduate four-year institutions (AAUP 1983).

When compensation at public and private institutions is compared, faculty members at public institutions earn higher salaries, on the average. Full professors as well as faculty members at all levels in business and management, engineering, and computer science earn, on the average, however, somewhat higher salaries at private institutions than at public ones (Jacobson 1983). In fact, salaries differ by discipline across many types of institutions. In 1982, new assistant professors in business, computer sciences, and engineering received salaries several thousand dollars higher than the average salary of new assistant professors at state colleges, while new assistant professors in foreign languages, history, and English were paid about $2,000 lower than the average (*Chronicle* 1982).

Using data from Ladd and Lipset's 1975 survey of the professoriate, Marsh and Dillon (1980) examined the relationship between faculty members' activities and the reward system. They found a positive relationship between amount of research and base salary and supplemental income, and between departmental and institutional involvement and base salary. In contrast, teaching activities were negatively correlated with both amount of base salary and supplemental income: Indeed, "base salary was more negatively correlated with hours spent teaching than it was positively related to numbers of books published" (p. 551). Their conclusion that teaching is not rewarded in higher education is consistent with the results of a 1973 survey in which a negative correlation was found between faculty salaries and amount of time spent teaching (McLaughlin, Montgomery, and Mahan 1979).

Research on salary and compensation is a complex matter, and few good models compare institutions (Batsche 1981). Nevertheless, the available data clearly demonstrate that the extrinsic rewards of faculty work, as expressed by salary level, have become less attractive over the last decade, and this trend is likely to continue for at least another decade (Carnegie Council 1980). While the particular combinations of attractive extrinsic and intrinsic rewards vary for faculty at different types of institutions (Smart 1978), all faculty are affected to some extent by the steady drop in financial compensation.

Intrinsic Dimensions in Faculty Work

Studies of faculty work "have focused on the outcomes of performance, rather than the explanation of actual performance behaviors. Thus, the study of research activity is virtually synonymous with the study of research productivity, as is teaching activity with teaching effectiveness" (Finkelstein 1978, p. 334). Studies of faculty members' satisfaction shed some light on the intrinsic factors in faculty work, however. Various studies of faculty members' satisfaction indicate that intrinsic aspects of their work are more important to faculty members than extrinsic motivators (McKeachie 1979). The intrinsic dimensions of faculty members' work that traditionally are important to faculty members, at least in terms of contribution to satisfaction, are autonomy and freedom (Eckert and Stecklein 1961; French, Tupper, and Mueller 1965; Gustad 1960; Pelz and Andrews 1976), intellectual interchange (Eckert and Stecklein 1961; Gustad 1960), and the opportunity to work with students (Eckert and Stecklein 1961; Wilson, Woods, and Gaff 1974).

Hackman and Oldham's model of job structure (1980), though it has been applied to academic work only recently (Bess 1981, 1982), could be very useful in clarifying the intrinsic nature of faculty members' work. Three "critical psychological states"—experienced meaningfulness of work, experienced responsibility for outcomes of the work, and knowledge of the actual results of the work activities—contribute to such outcomes as motivation, satisfaction, quality performance, and low turnover. Five "core job characteristics"—skill variety, task identity, task significance, autonomy, and feedback—lead to these three psychological states (Hackman and Oldham 1980). *Skill variety* refers to the variety of different activities involved in a job (p. 78). *Task identity* is defined as "the degree to which a job requires completion of a 'whole' and identifiable piece of work, that is, doing a job from beginning to end with a visible outcome" (p. 78). *Task significance* refers to the extent to which "the job has a substantial impact on the lives of other people" (p. 79). *Autonomy* refers to the degree of "freedom, independence, and discretion" that the job involves (p. 79). *Feedback* concerns the degree to which the job provides the employee with information about his or her effectiveness (p. 80).

Skill variety is fairly characteristic of the day-to-day work of faculty members. With responsibilities for research, teaching, and service, a professor can move from one activity to another when feeling the need for variety. Over a longer cycle, however, as opportunities for mobility decrease and pressures for productivity increase, faculty may find themselves doing the same things year after year. Those faculty seeking to increase their scholarly work for intrinsic reasons—not simply to meet the requirements of promotions committees—may feel the need to increase variety. Certainly, faculty development and retraining programs are attempts to encourage skill variety (while also broadening the pool of faculty available to perform highly demanded tasks in their institutions). The question of skill variety, then, is a complicated one. Objectively, it appears that academic work involves a good deal of variety. Subjectively, however, faculty members may experience it differently when they realize that they may be stuck in their institutions for the rest of their careers. Kanter's analyses (1977, 1978, 1979) of the opportunity and power structures within organizations imply, however, that efforts on the part of institutions to increase variety may be resisted by some faculty precisely because they feel stuck and embraced by others because they feel they have opportunities. In other words, as with many things, those who need it most want it least.

The solution to this dilemma lies in the degree to which faculty feel they have power over the things that matter to them. If workers feel they have control over their own work, the structure of broader institutional governance is not as important:

> *The type of control that is most important for alienation . . . is control, not over the product, but over the process of one's work. Ownership, hierarchical position, and division of labor have less effect on workers' feelings of alienation than do closeness of supervision, routinization, and substantive complexity* (Kohn 1976, pp. 126–27).

Faculty members' work has had considerable autonomy, especially in the past three decades. College teachers and researchers traditionally have been free to determine what they teach and study and how they go about it. Whether or not this autonomy is on the decline requires empirical testing, but there is no question that faculty members' influence on institutional policies is on the wane (Magarrell 1982b). If Kohn is correct in saying that workers are more concerned about immediate job characteristics than institutional ones, the problem may not be serious. Recent studies of faculty members' reactions as the balance of power shifts away from them, however, point to problems of declining morale (Anderson 1983; Cares and Blackburn 1978; Larkin and Clagett 1981). Given their professional status and their assumption of the right to participate in institutional governance on the basis of their expertise, faculty members may care as much about their institutional power as about their immediate job autonomy. This issue is complex, reflecting the coexistence of bureaucratic and collegial structures as well as the interdependence of professors' work and institutional policies.

Hackman and Oldham's concept of task identity, the degree to which a task involves following a project from start to finish, is somewhat difficult to assess in terms of faculty members' work. In one sense, a single instructor contributes only a small part to a student's development (Bess 1982). But in another sense, teaching a course involves organizing material on a particular topic into a package that can be studied in a term. From this perspective, teaching appears to have a high degree of "wholeness" or "task identity." Similarly, while faculty research may continually open new questions, the steps involved and the point of closure for any piece of research are under the control of the investigator. All told, task wholeness seems quite strong in the faculty member's work.

The degree of feedback in professors' work is hard to determine. The outcomes of teaching are notoriously difficult to assess, especially in the short-term designs that most researchers use, although recent efforts to measure the outcomes of education are attempting to do better (Forrest 1981; Whitla 1977; Winter, McClelland, and Stewart 1981). Despite difficulties in such assessments, professors do get some feedback from students' reactions to their lectures and from the results of examinations and other student work. Similarly, any immediate results from service provide some degree of feedback, though long-term effectiveness of service is as difficult to assess as is teaching. Research offers different sorts of feedback from teaching and service. Research activity does not provide much daily feedback unless it is conducted with others, but faculty receive feedback about their research from colleagues' reactions to professional presentations, reviewers' critiques, and ultimately publishers' decisions. How common it is for faculty to work with others on a scholarly project, compared with the solitary way most teach, is a subject worthy of some study, because it may be one source of greater vitality for them (Gaff 1983; Gamson forthcoming).

Studies of teaching and research, while plentiful, beg the question of significance in their emphasis on the measurement of productivity. Faculty members must assume that their contributions through research, teaching, and service are significant. The difficulty of evaluating specific outcomes of their work, however, also complicates the issue of significance. In an important sense, the whole enterprise of higher education is an assessment of the "task significance" of scholarly work. The study of this as well as other intrinsic dimensions of all three components of faculty work—teaching, scholarship, and service—has been neglected and requires considerable research.

Faculty Power and Participation in Organizational Decisions
"Formal binding power may lie with the administrator or the trustees, but a great deal of policy is initiated, formed, suggested or more generally influenced by the faculty" (Platt and Parsons 1970, p. 160). Faculty members, in fact, have more influence than power, influence that follows from their status as professionals rather than from their hierarchical position. Because their expertise legitimizes their claim to participation, it is not surprising that faculty members exert most influence on academic appointments and curriculum and least influence on financial matters (Baldridge et al. 1973; Kenen and Kenen 1978; Mortimer, Gunne, and Leslie 1976). Even in highly specialized departments where the faculty exercise considerable control over courses, selection of colleagues, and promotions and tenure, "the power of budget allocation is still reserved to the administrators" (Baldridge et al. 1973, p. 538).

According to a large survey of the late 1960s and early

1970s, faculty members perceived a "triumvirate of administration, department chairmen, and senior faculty . . . running the academic side of the institution, with senior faculty being replaced by trustees in matters of financial policy" (Kenen and Kenen 1978, p. 116). Senior faculty members were considered most influential, junior professors relatively powerless. Women faculty were perceived to be similar in influence to junior faculty except when they held high ranks (Kenen and Kenen 1978). A positive relationship existed between rank and credentials of faculty members and their influence (Ross 1977). Administrators perceived that "faculty influence over faculty appointments is positively related to productivity" (Ross 1977, p. 211). The relationship between rank and credentials with power strongly supports the assertion that status is the key determinant of faculty members' influence and power.

Many studies show that an institution's size and complexity are strongly related to faculty members' autonomy and power (Baldridge et al. 1973; Blau 1973; Boland 1971; Caplow and McGee 1958; Demerath, Stephens, and Taylor 1967; Kenen and Kenen 1978; Ross 1977; Stonewater 1977). Defining professional autonomy as "the ability of the faculty to set institutional goals and to structure the organization to maximize professional concerns," Baldridge et al. (1973) found larger institutions to have "more professional autonomy, fewer bureaucratic constraints, more individual influence for the academic professional, and greater freedom for disciplinary departments" (p. 536). One interpretation of this finding is that larger institutions have more specialized units. Faculty in such institutions therefore have a greater claim to external recognition and therefore to more power. Faculty at large universities are also engaged in research requiring direct negotiation with funding agencies, which gives them greater autonomy within their institutions (Caplow and McGee 1958; Demerath, Stephens, and Taylor 1967). Another explanation is that at larger institutions, the ratio of faculty to administrator is lower and the administration is thus less able to exert control over the faculty (Blau 1973).

Numerous studies indicate that faculty at more prestigious institutions exercise greater power and have more autonomy (Baldridge et al. 1973; Ecker 1973; Kenen and Kenen 1978; Light 1974; Parsons and Platt 1968). Again,

Faculty at more prestigious institutions exercise greater power and have more autonomy.

expertise seems to be the key variable. Faculty members at more prestigious institutions are likely to be recognized as experts in their areas of study. Because a department's reputation outside the institution is its source of power, "institutional and departmental authority is more collegial at professional schools and more hierarchical as one moves down the academic procession" (Light 1974, p. 21). When faculty appointments and promotions are to be decided, institutional quality is a major factor in determining the influence faculty will have. In the areas of financial and educational policy, however, differences in institutional quality do not seem as important (Finkelstein 1978, p. 316).

While a number of studies link institutional size, complexity, and quality to greater autonomy and power of faculty, not as much is known about differences in faculty members' power and participation according to institutional types. Based on data from the late 1960s and early 1970s, faculty members' influence "is deemed to be higher at public universities and private nondenominational institutions than at public colleges and denominational institutions" (Kenen and Kenen 1978, p. 121; see also Cares and Blackburn 1978).

External pressures and institutional responses to them may threaten professors' autonomy in the 1980s. "The ever-increasing role of outside agencies in campus matters is gradually wearing down internal governance structures" (Carnegie Foundation 1982, p. 89). Faculty power and participation are endangered: "Traditional structures do not seem to be working well. Faculty participation has declined. . . . The breakdown of campus governance is perhaps an all too predictable reaction to hard times. Life on a campus in retrenchment becomes tense" (Carnegie Foundation 1982, p. 74). A decade ago, faculty in larger schools may have experienced greater autonomy because institutional size acted as a "buffer" and insulation against environmental pressures and demands (Baldridge et al. 1973, p. 545). Today, however, faculty at even large institutions are feeling the effects of these pressures. The Institute of Higher Education at Columbia University recently completed a study of financial and educational trends in American higher education during the 1970s (Anderson 1983). The report used financial data collected for five academic years between 1967–68 and 1979–80 as well as faculty survey data collected in the late 1960s and early 1970s and again in 1979–80. Analyses of these data showed, overall, a sharp decline in faculty members' participation in governance. The proportion of faculty who believed that their campuses were characterized by the concept of "shared authority," with decisions determined jointly by the faculty and administration, declined from 64 percent in 1970 to 44 percent in 1980. While 52 percent of the respondents in 1970 agreed that faculty were widely involved in decisions about how the institution was run, only 45 percent believed it in 1980. Such changes, however, were not the same across all institutional types. Public research and doctoral universities and public comprehensive universities remained quite stable on these measures. Faculty at community colleges, on the other hand, reported a great decline in their participation in governance. The general conclusion of the study was that "campuses were governed less 'democratically' at the end of the decade than they were at the beginning" (Anderson 1983, p. 83).

It is not yet known the extent to which faculty members want to participate in decision making (Marshall 1976; Stonewater 1977; Touraine 1974). These questions should be considered: "How strong is the desire of faculty to participate in the actual shaping of policy? Is it likely that even those who sense and resent power would eschew this high degree of involvement and opt only to be able to challenge policies as issues arise on an ad hoc basis?" (Marshall 1976, p. 11). In answering these questions, care should be taken to distinguish among power, influence, autonomy, and participation, terms often used interchangeably and uncritically in the literature. Faculty usually recognize the differences, however. Some may resist participating in university committees because they want to be left alone to do their own work with a minimum of institutional interference; they value their autonomy. Others may feel that participation does not lead either to influence or power. Still others may prefer informal influence to formal participation. If participation and power are linked to faculty members' success and satisfaction and if lack of power is related to stress, then the current decline in instructors' participation could have serious negative effects.

Relationship to the Organization: Goal Congruence and Loyalty

The congruence between faculty members' goals and those of their institutions and the loyalty and commitment of faculty members to their universities and colleges are as yet largely unstudied. Because institutional goals are diverse, ambiguous, and sometimes contradictory (Baldridge et al. 1978; Cohen and March 1974; Kerr 1963), faculty often experience conflicting messages about which activities will be rewarded. Young faculty find that the institutions in which they manage to find jobs do not provide the conditions for carrying on the research they are required to produce for tenure. At the other extreme, faculty members who prefer teaching recognize that their institutions reward scholarship. While faculty members may agree with the general goals of their institutions and feel quite loyal, the potential for conflicts on particular issues is fairly high.

Several studies of faculty loyalty (Blau 1973; Kenen 1974; Lewis 1967; Nandi 1968; Parsons and Platt 1968; Razak 1969; Spencer 1969) point toward the conclusion that institutional loyalty depends on a faculty member's status in the institution, the profession, and the discipline (Finkelstein 1978). As status increases (as measured by age, length of service, rank, and tenure), loyalty to the institution increases. Organizational loyalty and professional commitment, however, appear to vary independently (Razak 1969). Senior professors actively involved in research can therefore express strong commitment to both the institution and the discipline. Faculty members at the highly prestigious, research-oriented institutions identify strongly with their discipline, by participating in professional associations, and with their departmental and institutional colleagues (Blau 1973; Parsons and Platt 1968).

The commitment of employees is crucial to the success of any organization; it could be a determining factor in the ability of colleges and universities to cope successfully with problems of finances and enrollment. Among the reasons for leaving an institution are negative assessments of administrative policy, perceptions of a deteriorating work situation, including increased workloads and neglected rewards, and a sense that support for faculty members' programs or departments is diminishing (Toombs and Marlier 1981). While these findings should not be generalized, it would be worthwhile to investigate those factors that lessen commitment to the point that professors decide to leave their institutions or even the academic profession. In a more positive perspective, one could learn more about the conditions under which professors agree to forgo salary and benefits to assist their ailing institutions.

Outcomes of Faculty Work
The outcomes of faculty work have been examined in terms of performance, satisfaction, and morale. No single predictor or group of predictors explains much of the variance in overall performance (Finkelstein 1978). One might expect job satisfaction or amount of time taken for professional leave to make a difference, but neither seems to be related to overall performance. The only personality trait that may relate to overall productivity is stress (Finkelstein 1978). Stress has different effects on different personalities; high stress is associated with reduced productivity in faculty members who are research-oriented, anxious, and less sociable, while it is related to increased productivity for individuals with opposite characteristics (Clark 1973). Factors relating to overall performance cannot be generalized, however; the more useful studies are those dealing with "specific dimensions of academic performance" (Finkelstein 1978, p. 253).

One dimension of academic performance is productivity as evidenced in research. It appears that "colleague climate as reflected in institutional quality together with an individual's own orientation toward research are the prime determinants of research productivity" (Finkelstein 1978, p. 262). Though institutional type and quality are both strong predictors of research productivity (Finkelstein 1978), quality of the institution is the more important predictor (Fulton and Trow 1974). "Faculty at high quality colleges were at least as productive as faculty at mid-level universities" (Finkelstein 1978, p. 256).

The weight of research in decisions about promotion at high-quality institutions directly affects the choice of new faculty (Blau 1973). Thus, in Blau's study, professors were selected as colleagues if they demonstrated qualifications for research compatible with the institution's expectations, and a faculty member's feeling of obligation to do research and the weight assigned to scholarship in decisions about tenure had only an indirect effect on involvement in research. In the same study, the colleague climate (the percentage of the faculty holding a doctorate) and the individual's possession of a doctorate accounted for 30 percent of the observed variance in involvement in research. In another study, a professor's interest in research and interaction with colleagues doing research explained 60 percent of the variance in productivity (Behymer 1974). These factors were more salient than such extrinsic factors as the faculty member's perception of the pressure to publish.

In these and numerous other studies, "institutional quality/colleague climate and individual professional characteristics associated with a research orientation emerged as the most powerful predictors of publication activity" (Finkelstein 1978, p. 262). Studies of the relationship between departmental characteristics and publication activity indicate that the quality of the department (measured by reputation and the proportion of colleagues holding doctorates) is the most important predictor. The nature of administrative leadership and size of the department are not very important (Finkelstein 1978).

The "productive" faculty member thus holds a doctorate, places a strong value on research, and started publishing early. He or she spends more time in research than teaching, has little commitment to administrative work, and stays in close contact with colleagues and developments in the discipline (Finkelstein 1978). As more faculty attempt to emulate this pattern under the pressure to publish, it is little wonder that participation in institutional governance has been declining.

Across disciplines, natural scientists are most productive, followed by social scientists, and finally by faculty in the humanities, education, and the fine arts (Finkelstein 1978). One factor may be differences in how natural scientists, social scientists, and humanists communicate their scholarly work (Biglan 1971; Roe 1972). Humanities faculty write books; natural scientists write journal articles. While multiple authorships are common in the natural sciences and fairly usual in the social sciences, single authorship is the mode in the humanities. Perhaps differences in productivity between disciplines would not seem great if more weight were given to books and articles authored by a single person (Finkelstein 1978).

Even after tenure and promotion are no longer concerns, faculty members continue to publish. While this pattern may indicate scholars' internal motivation to engage in scholarly work, rank does seem to be an important predictor of the rate of productivity in research (Finkelstein 1978). Perhaps those higher in rank publish faster because professors of higher rank may have more control over the amount of their workload (Fulton and Trow 1974). They also may have more contacts and the know-how to get them through the publishing process. A third possibility is that those at higher ranks already have a strong publishing record, which continues at their new rank.

The relationship between age and productivity in research follows a saddle-shaped curve, with the specific pattern depending on discipline and institutional quality (Bayer and Dutton 1977; Blackburn, Behymer, and Hall 1978; Fulton and Trow 1974; Pelz and Andrews 1976; Roe 1972). During his early career, the young professor devotes considerable effort to research, pursuing interests started in graduate school that are likely to pay off in tenure. This period of productivity dips as associate professorship is reached and then increases again when full professorship is gained (Blackburn, Behymer, and Hall 1978). Bayer and Dutton (1977) report a more continuous decline in research productivity five to ten years into the career. At elite institutions, age is not associated with a decline in productivity (Fulton and Trow 1974). Interests may shift with age; as professors get older, their priorities for research shift from specific, empirical studies to theoretical, interdisciplinary studies (Parsons and Platt 1968).

The effectiveness of teaching and service is very difficult to assess. Studies attempting to measure the effectiveness of teaching are difficult to compare because they use different measurements and criteria and are usually based on research in a single institution, and studies of the effectiveness of service are nonexistent. These methodological problems aside, productivity in research and the effectiveness of teaching seem quite independent (Finkelstein 1978). When the effectiveness of teaching is measured by the intellectual competence demonstrated by the faculty member (a criterion often used by faculty), "research productivity and the expertise it engenders or the general ability which it signals does bear a fairly small, but consistently positive, relationship to good teaching. To the extent that judgments of teaching are based on socio-emotional aspects of a learning situation (and students appear more disposed to this criterion), then the expertise developed in a research activity appears a largely irrelevant factor" (Finkelstein 1978, p. 288). Time spent in research apparently does not detract from teaching responsibilities. Extra time for research is taken from professors' leisure and family activities rather than from teaching duties (Harry and Goldner 1972).

That good research is both a necessary and sufficient condition for good teaching . . . is not resoundingly supported by the evidence. Resoundingly disconfirmed, however, is the notion that research involvement detracts from good teaching by channeling professorial time and effort away from the classroom (Finkelstein 1978, pp. 288–89).

Faculty members' satisfaction as an outcome of work has been studied extensively since the late 1960s. Much of the work has been modeled on studies of motivation and satisfaction in government and industry (Finkelstein 1978). Several recent studies suggest that satisfaction among faculty is relatively high. Forty-three percent of the respondents in one study said they "liked" their position, and an additional 46 percent said they liked it "very much" (Bennett and Griffitt 1976, p. 2). In another study, 85 percent of the respondents indicated that they were satisfied or very satisfied, a result almost identical to responses to the same question in 1968 but a drop from 93 percent in 1956 (Willie and Stecklein 1981). Disaggregated, the 1980 figures show a decline from 1968 in the percentage who reported they were very satisfied in four-year institutions, with more saying they were just satisfied, indifferent, and dissatisfied.

Early research found no significant relationships between faculty members' satisfaction and rank, career age, chronological age, length of service, highest degree, or salary (Hill 1965; Theophilus 1967). More recently, researchers report that satisfaction increases with rank on several items: tenure and promotion, opportunity for input into policies, allocation of resources to departments, and the location of the university (Bennett and Griffitt 1976). In contrast, satisfaction with fringe benefits decreases with rank.

While several studies look at the effects of extrinsic and intrinsic factors, such as work conditions and tasks performed, on faculty members' job satisfaction (Avakian 1971; Eckert and Williams 1972; Leon 1973; Swierenga 1970; Whitlock 1965), the lack of multivariate analyses in these studies makes it difficult to sort out the precise impact of different factors (Finkelstein 1978). Nevertheless, intrinsic factors generally seem more significant than extrinsic factors in explaining professors' satisfaction. A study of faculty at a large public university found that the area of greatest satisfaction was the "general atmosphere or surroundings" (Bennett and Griffitt 1976, p. 2). Five items measured this concept: the academic characteristics of the typical students, the quality of departmental colleagues, the quality of the university's faculty in general, the opportunity for interactions outside the department or discipline, and the community in which the institution was located. The factors that seem to bring the most satisfaction to faculty include feelings of academic freedom, the nature of the work itself (responsibility, challenge, variety), relations with competent employees, job stability (tenure), and professional and social recognition (Bess 1981). Autonomy, academic freedom, and independence are among the most frequently mentioned items contributing to satisfaction (Winkler 1982). More than a decade ago, research found that satisfaction increased as respondents perceived they were participating in decision making (Barrett 1969). The opportunity to work with students is also a very important intrinsic source of satisfaction (Bess 1981; Cohen 1973; Willie and Stecklein 1981; Winkler 1982).

While intrinsic factors may be particularly important for faculty members' job satisfaction, extrinsic factors "may be more important determinants of job *dis*satisfaction" (Finkelstein 1978, p. 228). Respondents in the Theophilus study (1967) expressed more dissatisfaction with material incentives than with intrinsic incentives. In another study, tasks and conditions of work were most important in contributing to job satisfaction, but salary and faculty/administrative relationships contributed to job *dis*satisfaction (Eckert and Williams 1972). Salary seems to be one of the single greatest sources of dissatisfaction (Edmundson 1969; Ladd 1979; Winkler 1982), but poor administration and leadership, lack of support (public support, equipment, budget, secretarial), and the university's structure and reward system are other important sources of dissatisfaction (Winkler 1982). Low satisfaction is associated with limited opportunities for promotion and advancement, limited prospects for comfortable retirement, and limited prospects for financial security (Bureau of Institutional Research 1974). Limited time can also cause stress and unhappiness (Clark and Blackburn 1973; Edmundson 1969).

While considerable research has examined the conditions under which faculty have the greatest power and participate most in decision making, less attention has been devoted to the relationship between these variables and the satisfaction and productivity of faculty members. An exploratory study suggests that participation and power may be very important to faculty members' success (Cares and Blackburn 1978). A strong relationship existed between faculty members' perceptions of the extent of democracy in their departments and control of the environment (defined as the ability to influence practices and policies relating to their work) and their success and satisfaction. A more recent study found that stress among community college professors was related to "not being involved in the decision making, being treated like children, and overdoing the use of restrictions and regulations to solve problems" (Larkin and Clagett 1981, p. 3). These studies suggest that lack of power and opportunities for participation in decision making may have quite negative effects on faculty members' satisfaction.

The overall conclusion about faculty satisfaction from the research to date is that "faculty tend to derive more satisfaction from the nature of their work itself, while they tend to express dissatisfaction most frequently with extrinsic factors, such as salary [and] administrative leadership . . ." (Finkelstein 1978, p. 229). As yet, the research does not explain why this observation is so, nor does it satisfactorily address the question of the relationship between satisfaction and productivity. "Satisfaction/dissatisfaction may not be a unidimensional construct, but may rather exist as two separate continua subject to unique sets of determinants" (Finkelstein 1978, p. 229).

The few studies that have examined professors' satisfaction with the academic career generally agree that faculty seem quite satisfied with their careers, regardless of institutional type or their age or sex (DeVries 1970; Gaff and Wilson 1975; Willie and Stecklein 1981). One study, comparing the responses of faculty in two-year and four-year institutions in 1956, 1968, and 1980 showed a decline from 1968 to 1980 in the percentage who said they would choose to work in an educational institution if they had the opportunity to decide again (Willie and Stecklein 1981). Of community college faculty, 82 percent answered affirmatively in 1968, compared to 71 pecent in 1980. Among faculty at four-year institutions, the percentage of respondents in 1968 saying they would choose the same career was 86 percent, compared to 72 percent in 1980. While most faculty find their teaching to be satisfying, scholarly activity seems to provide more satisfaction to natural and social scientists than to humanities and professional faculty (Gaff and Wilson 1975). Only Cares (1975) found significant differences in levels of professors' satisfaction with career. The more "self-actualized" faculty, those who felt they participated extensively in decision making, and those who felt they had greater influence in the institution experienced higher satisfaction. Satisfaction with one's career may thus be more highly related to a professor's personality and perceptions of the career than to professional status or the employing institution's status (Finkelstein 1978).

The morale of faculty has been given much less attention. Satisfaction and morale are clearly different. Satisfaction refers to one's personal contentment and sense of well-being, whereas morale relates more to one's relationship to an organization. Morale is based on such factors as pride in the organization and its goals, faith in its leadership, and a sense of shared purpose with and loyalty to others in the organization. Collective morale can be low at the same time that personal satisfaction is high (Hunter, Ventimiglia, and Crow 1980, p. 29). But morale among professors is suffering from some of the same factors that diminish satisfaction, particularly faculty members' involvement in decision making and planning. In one study, the percentage of faculty members who indicated that their morale was high fell from 61 percent in 1970 to 51 percent in 1980 (Anderson 1983). Public research and doctorate-granting universities and public comprehensive universities did not experience this drop, however. The drop in morale was most apparent at public community colleges, precisely those institutions where "professors believe that their opinions on college operations are considered less . . . [and] faculty have less confidence in administration . . ." (p. 111).

This seeming contradiction between the reports of general satisfaction and professors' frequently mentioned complaints and dissatisfactions may have a simple explanation: "To indicate otherwise, especially in the face of the present interinstitutional immobility in the profession, is to admit that the choice of occupation and institution was a poor life decision, now virtually irrevocable . . ." (Bess 1981, p. 29). The pressures of the 1980s may force faculty back to more basic needs like security and salary; thus, they may become "a new class of 'alienated' workers" (Bess 1981, p. 28). This shift may be expressed in more participation in unions or institutional governance or in "the sacrifice of quality for quantity in the striving to secure adequate rewards" (p. 28). At the same time, however, because intrinsic rewards seem highly related to faculty members' satisfaction, they may be able to tolerate considerable stress without a great loss of motivation (p. 35).

Summary

The problems facing higher education today are making academic life far from idyllic. Faculty are experiencing stress from a decline in extrinsic rewards and increased workloads. The strong intrinsic motivation characteristic of college faculty seems to be threatened. Pressures for more productivity come at the same time that the faculty's power in their institutions is declining. These forces are operating unevenly across disciplines, types of institutions, and levels of prestige. Indeed, the very existence of such variation within and between institutions may be a source of the vulnerability of the academic profession in the face of external pressures on higher education. The effects of these pressures on salary levels, job security, participation in governance, and opportunity for career growth merit close attention in the years ahead.

THE WORK EXPERIENCE OF ADMINISTRATORS

"Administrator" is a broad term that includes presidents and vice presidents, deans and department chairs, admissions directors, financial aid directors, and student personnel counselors. All of them are likely to experience the university workplace in different ways. The organizational structure of the university or college and current external pressures affect the nature of administrators' work. (Tables II, III, and IV in the appendix summarize the recent research on the work experience of presidents, mid-level administrators, and other administrators, respectively.)

Senior Administrators

The university president is at once a friend of students, a colleague of faculty members, and a good fellow who associates with the alumni (Kerr 1963). By the mid-1970s, however, the demands on presidents weighed more heavily.

> *A key problem of the president today is how to be accountable, be in compliance with an assortment of external regulations, satisfy the governing board that he or she is providing leadership to meet the current crises and the needs of the future, and, at the same time, accommodate the expectations of participation and consultation implied by most internal governance. The pressures that flow from this quandary are relentless and often disabling. To please the governing board is to displease the faculty. To satisfy the faculty is to engender hostility in the legislature, and on and on* (Kauffman 1980, p. 79).

"The role, function, and structure of the college presidency have undergone dramatic changes. No longer is it a position of stability and seclusion from an increasingly complex world" (Buxton, Pritchard, and Buxton 1976, p. 79).

Extrinsic factors in presidents' work

Presidents' activities and role. A variety of metaphors have been advanced to describe the role of a university or college president—a politician (particularly a mayor), a business executive (Cohen and March 1974), a super entrepreneur, a symphony orchestra conductor (Kauffman

1980), a zookeeper, and the operator of a dispensing machine (Monson 1967). These terms suggest the diverse functions, constituencies—and frustrations—to which presidents are subjected.

The functions a new president assumes are significantly related to the "type of institution, its history, traditions, and ethos" (Kauffman 1980, p. 41). While the American Council on Education offers seminars for new presidents, no other training is available to prepare a person for the role. How does a new president learn the responsibilities of the role? Chief academic officers traditionally have had a background as faculty and have learned how to be a president on the job.

In part, the expectations about the new president's performance in the role will be determined by social norms, rules, differing perspectives, the performances of previous presidents, and especially by the actor's perception of the expectations of those who observe and react to the performance (Kauffman 1980, p. 41).

The actual tasks and functions of the president can be subdivided into several basic areas. One set of tasks relates to the president's responsibilities for leadership: Senior officers must keep in mind broad vision for the institution and continually shape the institution's goals. A second area of responsibility involves a "representational, communication, and interpretation function" (Kauffman 1980, p. 13): The president is expected to articulate the essence and value of the institution. The third task involves management and responsibility for control of the institution as a whole (Kauffman 1980).

Presidents may be chosen for their ability to handle a particular difficulty, but they discover quite soon that efforts to effect change ignite considerable resistance. A new president becomes aware very quickly that the position involves grappling with conflicting expectations from different constituencies (Kauffman 1980). While college presidents may think success depends upon political skill, chief academic officers may stress attention to fiscal issues and educational programs, business officers to promoting growth and sound fiscal conditions, and alumni, community leaders, trustees, faculty, and students to the president's acting as a symbol of the institution (Cohen and March 1974).

Every president must become accustomed to pleasing some constituencies while disappointing others, and political skill is an important ingredient of a president's success. Campus presidents in statewide systems, for example, must implement decisions of the central governing board at the same time they must represent the interests of their campus. Their faculty may view them as too responsive to the central board, while the board may find them too uncooperative.

Presidents spend a great deal of time in work-related activities. New presidents, who try to make themselves available to everyone while also learning the intricacies of their responsibilities, report feeling especially severe demands on their time (Kauffman 1980). Limited time is in fact one of the less desirable extrinsic aspects of a president's job. Sources of dissatisfaction include a "lack of opportunity for teaching and conducting research" (Buxton, Pritchard, and Buxton 1976, p. 81) and a lack of time for work, family, and leisure (Buxton, Pritchard, and Buxton 1976; Solomon and Tierney 1977). "One [president] . . . suggested that he spends too much of his 14-hour day in dealing with 'matters which are peripheral to the academic goals of the college' " (Buxton, Pritchard, and Buxton 1976, p. 81).

Presidents spend between 50 and 55 hours on work-related activities from Monday through Friday and another five to ten hours over the weekend (Cohen and March 1974). Despite the long hours, however, their schedules do not require that they always be in the office. Work may be conducted at home, out of town, or through a president's many social engagements. Administrative work involving specific decisions is more likely to occur early in the day and early in the week, and more political interactions happen more often in the latter part of the day and the week. The specific pattern of allocation is related to several factors. One is the size of the institution. Presidents at larger schools appear to exhibit a more "local," less "cosmopolitan" focus in their activities. Another factor is the expectation throughout the academic culture and presidents' own expectations that professors—and therefore presidents—generally work 60-hour weeks. Because presi-

The president is expected to articulate the essence and value of the institution.

dential success cannot be linked to any specific behavior, the very ambiguity of expectations leads presidents to work long hours. Finally, presidents are often individuals who have achieved their position partly because they enjoy hard work (Cohen and March 1974).

Opportunity structure. Presidents have reached their posts from a variety of trajectories and experiences during their careers. Only a very small number of presidents follow completely the normative career trajectory in which an individual moves from faculty member to department chair to dean, provost, and president (Moore 1983a, 1983b, 1983c; Moore et al. 1983). Many skip rungs or include other experiences in their career paths. Once individuals do assume the helm, however, they do not experience security; they do indeed serve "at the pleasure of the board" (Kauffman 1980). The average term of office is between five and eight years (Cohen and March 1974; Nason 1980b). Because a presidency is the pinnacle of an academic career, few comparable new positions are available. After leaving the presidency, 14 percent of the respondents in one survey took another position in academic administration, usually lower in status, prestige, and power. Ten percent took positions in government, business, and nonprofit organizations, and the rest went back to positions as faculty members or clergy. Many presidents expressed the feeling that they did not have good alternatives after the presidency (Cohen and March 1974). "Many college and university presidents may be serving at the displeasure of the board, but, because of board inertia, are perhaps hanging on, feeling trapped in their positions, and would leave if they could find any suitable place to go" (Kauffman 1980, p. ix).

Reward structure. The salary levels for academic executive officers are not as high as might be expected, given the pressures of the work. The median salary of chief executive officers of universities and colleges of all types in 1982–83 was $55,624. For presidents at all universities, the median was $67,760, at four-year colleges $54,000, and at two-year colleges $50,000. Executive vice presidents during the same time period earned a median salary of $49,000 at all institutions, but the median salary differed considerably when institutional types were compared. At all universities taken together, the median salary was $56,000, at four-year colleges $41,000, and at two-year colleges $46,066 (*Chronicle* 1983a). Salaries in higher education are considerably lower than salaries for comparable positions in business. University and college presidents are paid less than one-half the salaries of chief executive officers in business (Bowen 1978). Furthermore, college and university presidents are expected to contribute to various organizations and charities as well as to subsidize their college-related entertainment. While a university-owned president's home appears to be a desirable benefit associated with the position, it can be a financial drain if the president's family must pay for daily housekeeping expenses, including utilities. On the other hand, if the president's family does not pay for utilities, it often feels pressured by budget watchers to keep costs down.

Recognizing that financial remuneration is minimal for all that the position of president involves, Kauffman (1980) urges that college and university presidents be highly respected for the service they perform:

> *We must restore the concept of service to the role of the presidency. The incentives of honor, security, or material gain are simply not there any longer, if they ever existed. . . . Only the concept of service can be an appropriate incentive* (p. 1).

Intrinsic dimensions in presidents' work

Not the least drawback of living in an official president's house is the sense of living in a fishbowl. Presidents and their families live under constant scrutiny (Kauffman 1980). Coupled with this factor is the great loneliness of the job. The president cannot please all faculty members, students, trustees, and alumni. Because of their own socialization and identity as faculty members, presidents may feel particular pain when faculty and students disagree with them.

But the position has its intrinsic rewards, and, on the whole, presidents are "healthy, positive, energetic people who regard their work as useful and even important" (Kauffman 1980, p. 84). High status certainly compensates.

The president usually occupies impressive quarters and is surrounded by staff to help with most aspects of the job. The presidency is considered the peak of an academic career. The chief executive officer is seen as "heroic," the person who makes decisions, assumes wide responsibilities, and guides the institution (Cohen and March 1974, p. 79). Though all university and college presidents have high status, the degree of status associated with a presidency depends more on the institution's quality than on the quality of the president (Cohen and March 1974).

Feedback is an important intrinsic dimension of work. Presidents rarely have a clear sense of the specific expectations they should meet or the criteria under which they will be judged.

> *Not only do presidents often not know what is expected of them but they are also too often judged on inconsistent or contradictory standards. . . . Trustees think that they make clear to the presidents-elect what is needed and expected, but the presidents report that they are too often left in the dark* (Nason 1980a, p. 32).

The power exercised by presidents

Because of their position, presidents exercise a high degree of professional autonomy and hold much power. The strength of a president's power, however, depends on the degree to which the board delegates authority (Kauffman 1980). When a board and a president agree on expectations, the president can exercise power with more autonomy. But in recent years, several factors have been eroding presidential power.

> *. . . We in higher education have gradually eliminated considerable areas of presidential judgment and discretion by adopting uniform procedures, formulas, and policies that command our fealty more than does our good sense* (Kauffman 1980, p. 109).

State and federal regulations weaken the autonomy of campus officials. State legislative bodies and coordinating boards constrain the power of presidents, particularly in public institutions. Systemwide unions often circumvent the campus president and deal directly with the governor or legislature. As a result of the process of centralization, campus chancellors in some state systems "have been demoted to middle-level managers" (Kauffman 1980, p. 71).

There is growing centralization of authority and decision making. This trend affects faculty governance on the campus level and many system administrators have seen the election of collective bargaining by the faculty as a result. Faculty organization further justifies centralization and strengthens the need for a system office and staff, in addition to strengthening the role of state officials in higher education governance. The greater involvement of the state in higher education, in turn, increases systemization and bureaucratization of decision making, altering the role of the campus administrator and making it seem less personally significant and rewarding (Kauffman 1980, p. 64).

University and college presidents experience their power in an observable pattern as they progress through their years in office. New executive officers tend to overestimate their power; early mistakes tend to curb this view. As they begin to recognize their limits, however, they simultaneously gain legitimacy, which increases their power. If they are effective in fund raising and in interactions with their board or the legislature, and as they take strong leadership positions, their power grows more (Cohen and March 1974; Kauffman 1980). They must achieve a delicate balance: They must recognize the limits of the office, yet "failure to use influence on important matters becomes a sign of weakness and has its costs" (Kauffman 1980, p. 48).

Presidents can exercise more power in some areas than in others. They may exhibit strong leadership in establishing budgetary priorities, long-range planning, personnel policy and selection, program development, and the physical plant. Their role is usually not as pronounced in decisions concerning the quality of faculty, the core curricula, and teaching (Kauffman 1980, p. 49). In those areas, the faculty remains strong.

Outcomes of presidents' work
The challenges of the work itself appear to account for much of the general satisfaction presidents report. Their

satisfaction is derived from such tasks as "averting disaster, saving blood, retaining funding levels, rescuing the system from financial disaster, avoiding cutbacks, and resolving hard differences constructively" (Kanter 1979, p. 3). Among the positive aspects of their work, presidents of state-controlled colleges and universities list "the challenging nature of their work" and "their role in the community and state" (Buxton, Pritchard, and Buxton 1976, p. 85).

Professional autonomy is the source of greatest satisfaction (Buxton, Pritchard, and Buxton 1976). Presidents are very satisfied with their "freedom and independence," with the "power and prestige associated with the office," and with "presidential participation in institutional policy formulation" (Buxton, Pritchard, and Buxton 1976, pp. 81–85). Similarly, satisfaction and power, influence, challenge, responsibility, and autonomy are related positively (Solomon and Tierney 1977). Presidents are also satisfied with the "intellectual and social nature of the office," the "opportunity to improve the quality of life in the world," and the "opportunity to shape the future of their institutions" (Buxton, Pritchard, and Buxton 1976, p. 85). They derive great satisfaction from their relationships with students, faculty, and administrators.

Some of the dissatisfaction presidents experience is closely related to the external pressures on colleges and universities. The chancellors or presidents of campuses in state systems appear to "have the most complaints about lack of satisfaction in their positions" (Kauffman 1980, p. 70). The governance structure of the system constrains their authority and often forces them into situations of severely conflicting demands. Presidents are particularly concerned about the economic problems associated with declining enrollments and changing state and federal appropriations (Buxton, Pritchard, and Buxton 1976). They do not particularly like fund raising and handling financial affairs, yet it is likely that they will be required to do more. The limited time associated with the position is a source of dissatisfaction. Finally, executive officers are not satisfied with "the amount of recognition that academic presidents receive from members of other professions" (Buxton, Pritchard, and Buxton 1976, p. 83).

While the presidency offers an opportunity to make a major impact on a college or university and on higher education more broadly and while it provides considerable satisfactions, it also is a position of pressure, challenge, and conflict. As outside forces intensify, senior officers of universities and colleges may gain power as decision making becomes more centralized, but they cannot help also experiencing heightened tension and perhaps less satisfaction. Because strong, creative leaders are vital for the success of colleges and universities, the experience of presidents should continue to be studied. Vice presidents too play an important role, and they have been the focus of very little research to date.

Middle Administrators

Scott's phrase (1979c) "robots or reinsmen" captures the fundamental dilemma that faces middle-level administrators. Dubbed "lords, squires, and yeomen" (Scott 1978), middle administrators include directors and deans of support services and other administrative personnel to whom assistants and first-line supervisors report. Presidents and provosts, academic deans, and librarians are not included in this category. Forces within and without higher education have contributed to an increase in the number and type of middle administrative positions, with the specific type at any particular college or university usually a function of the institution's size and complexity (Scott 1978). Affirmative action officers, institutional researchers, counselors for specific constituencies, and government relations specialists, though once unusual, can now be found on many campuses.

Middle administrators sometimes must act as "robots," exhibiting only "programmed behavior," when some would prefer to be the "reinsmen" who exercise their talents from behind the scene (Scott 1979c, p. 17).

They enter the career field to work with students, but find that they work mostly with paper. They have high institutional loyalty, but must look off-campus for training, guidance, recognition, colleagueship, and rewards. They are highly oriented to service, but find increasing pressures to exert both administrative and financial controls. They have little substantial contact with faculty and senior officers, but want higher status on campus. They exhibit highly desired traits of behavior—tolerance of ambiguity, administrative talent, fiscal ability, and interpersonal skills—but experience a very high rate of turnover (Scott 1979b, p. 93).

Middle managers are required to interact with many constituencies within higher education—faculty, other administrators, the president and executive officers, trustees, and students. Middle administrators occupy a peculiar role in the university because of their responsibilities to these various groups and to the "mixed organizational structure" within higher education. Acting as "linking pins" between vertical and horizontal levels, middle managers implement but seldom develop policy (Scott 1978). Their positions force them to face the conflict between "service for others versus control of others and their actions" (Scott 1978, p. 1). At the same time, they are expected "to be servants to students and faculty, and instruments of institutional policy set by senior administrators and trustees. They are to be both servants (as support staff) and policemen (as monitors of procedures)" (Scott 1979c, p. 20).

Activities and workload. Middle managers in any organization usually have diverse functions, and they "contribute the essential knowledge without which the key decisions cannot be made, at least not effectively" (Drucker 1973, p. 450). Similarly, "mid-level administrators perform their tasks in support of an institution's goals and in control of its activities" (Scott 1978, p. 6). They often serve as liaison with the "suppliers of resources," they coordinate and implement the allocation of resources and various activities within the institution, and they often work directly with students (Scott 1978, p. 5). Like faculty, administrators find that lack of time is a source of frustration, an issue that is undoubtedly related to other frustrations, such as not enough staff, limited resources, and too much paperwork (Scott 1978).

"The functions performed, the organization of functions, and the specialization of functions vary by the size and complexity of the institution" (Scott 1978, p. 7). Specific tasks also vary, of course, depending on the office (for example, admissions, financial aid, institutional research) the administrator occupies. Smaller colleges may combine offices like admissions and registration rather than establish two separate positions. At a small college, the senior administrator's secretary may handle personnel matters; in contrast, at a large university, personnel work may involve many employees handling counseling, staff development, organizational analysis and development, and other activities (Scott 1978).

With increasing size of an institution, tasks become more specialized, at least for admissions officers and probably for others (Scott 1976b, 1978; Vinson 1977). In recent years, admissions officers have devoted more time to staff supervision than to actual admissions work. They are also less likely to be involved in tangential activities like registration and financial aid (Vinson 1977). This trend toward specialization increases the professionalization of middle administrators (Scott 1978).

Opportunity structure. Opportunity structure for administrators in higher education is limited (Kanter 1979; Scott 1978, 1979c). With few places at the top and affirmative action guidelines that often necessitate searches for people beyond those already employed in the lower ranks, middle managers tend to remain in their positions for a long time. Directors have less mobility than assistants and associates, but as long as they remain, their subordinates have less opportunity to advance in the institution (Scott 1979c).

"The professional staff office appeared to be, or was, in the process of change from the . . . generalist in a position with limited career opportunities . . . to a more specialized, academically credentialed individual who views higher education administration as a profession and as a step in a personal career" (Anselm 1980, p. 200). Attrition may occur in the face of dead-end careers. If talented administrators are to be retained in higher education, colleges and universities must offer them new kinds of opportunities and challenges.

Reward structure. Little evidence shows that salary incentives can compensate for restricted opportunity and comparatively low status. Though middle administrators in universities and colleges have comparable skills to their counterparts in business and industry, where salary scales may reach a high level, the salaries for many academic mid-level administrators are quite low. In 1982–83, median salaries for administrators at all universities in such mid-level positions as manager of the payroll, director of student activities, associate director of food services, director of accounting, director of annual giving, and director of the academic computing center ranged from approximately $20,000 to $30,000. Assistants to the president of a university or college earned a median salary of $30,632, across all institutions. As the highest paid academic middle administrators, assistants to the president of a system, however, earned $36,000. The salary level of these assistants is noticeably higher than that of most middle administrators (*Chronicle* 1983b). In the face of severe budgetary constraints, salary increases are sometimes given to only select employee groups in a university or college. Declining morale and resentment can result when the faculty is favored over middle administrators for salary increases. Differences in status are apparent in the more intangible rewards. While administrators must handle the tasks like admission and registration that support the faculty's work, they receive neither the formal responsibilities nor the rewards bestowed on faculty members. Many are invisible workers who are sometimes passed over in such institutional social rituals as presidential receptions (Scott 1979c).

Intrinsic dimensions in middle administrators' work
The intrinsic characteristics of the middle administrator's work have never been studied. Variety in work is one of the most important characteristics for a satisfying, motivating job (Hackman and Oldham 1980). Whether variety characterizes the work of middle administrators is difficult to determine independent of the particular job being performed. One would expect that directors and associate and assistant directors of an administrative office would have a sufficiently diverse range of tasks to ensure variety in their work. The trend toward specialization in administrative jobs, however, may reduce variety, if indeed it is characteristic.

The literature focuses especially on the tensions inherent in the relationship between faculty and administrators (Baumgartel 1976; Scott 1978; Thomas 1978). Faculty show little respect for administrators and resist accepting them as full members of the academic community. Observing tension between faculty and mid-level administrative staff in her study at a large university, Anselm (1980) asserts that "the relationship between professional staff and faculty was not organizationally defined and the potential for a conflict between them was evident" (p. 199). This tension has an obvious structural reason: Faculty members, oriented to their respective disciplines, may see issues differently from administrators, who are more oriented toward the bureaucratic structure. Middle administrators seem to be more comparable to business people in their backgrounds, orientations, and training (Hauser and Lazarsfeld 1964; Scott 1976a), but it also appears that middle administrators value collegial ideals (though faculty members may not see it) (Bess 1978; Scott 1978). The specific professional interests of mid-level administrators reflect the kind and frequency of their interaction with faculty, the conditions of their employment, and their institutions' incentives (Bess 1978; Scott 1978).

Faculty show little respect for administrators and resist accepting them as full members of the academic community.

Professional status rests on control over a body of knowledge, and the "science of administration" remains at a rudimentary stage of development. Many middle administrators have advanced degrees (Scott 1976a) but get their specific training on the job (Scott 1978). The increasing specialization of administrative work as institutions grow has contributed to the professionalization of academic middle managers (Scott 1978; Vinson 1977). Some middle administrators—admissions officers, financial aid officers, institutional researchers, student personnel officers—have formed well-respected regional and national professional organizations. These organizations lobby, develop and disseminate materials to their constituents, conduct research, and organize conferences.

Within their institutions, however, administrators are more likely to derive their status from sources other than their role as professionals—their access to resources, in particular. The position of chief financial officer, for example, is gaining in prestige (Setoodeh 1981). Current financial pressures have brought new status and power to some administrators.

The issue of middle administrators' status is further complicated by shifts in the chain of command. The number of middle administrators has increased with the expansion of institutional size and complexity during the last several decades (Scott 1978). Many middle managers report to individuals whose status in the hierarchy has dropped as new bureaucratic levels have been added. The status of the administrators lower in the hierarchy declines accordingly. Furthermore, when supervisors have not risen through the ranks, they may not understand their subordinates' frustrations.

Power and participation in organizational decisions

The autonomy and power of middle administrators are difficult to assess. Middle administrators, unlike faculty, do not have the freedom to determine their work. Their work *is* rather the work of the institution, but from this situation they gain considerable influence.

Mid-level administrators hold considerable authority and have the knowledge to implement policies within their specific spheres, but they generally have little power to make broad institutional policy (Scott 1978). In contrast, the directors of major administrative departments and the assistants to the chief officers—the "professional staff members"—at a major midwestern public research university were perceived by both administrators and faculty as "holding substantial power to influence the administration of . . . policies" (Anselm 1980, p. 196). The two arguments are not really contradictory. Mid-level administrators do not have the power to *make* institutional policy, but their daily responsibilities give them access to privileged information. The way in which they organize and present this information to senior administrators or faculty committees can have considerable influence. Furthermore, as they administer decisions made by others, they can shape policy in practice. Anselm (1980) found in fact that a majority of the middle administrators and faculty members who responded to her survey believed that "the primary basis of professional staff power was found in the professional staff's role as information broker" (p. 146).

Like women, minorities, and other employees whose power is restricted (Kanter 1978), mid-level administrators are required to acquiesce to those who hold more power. Both administrators and faculty in Anselm's study (1980) agreed that mid-level administrators should *not* be part of the academic governance system (defined as the university senate and faculty committees). In this situation, administrative staff develop ways in their own sphere to deal with limitations on their power: "The professional staff survived by playing a role that reflected the subservant's political acumen and which exercised power while denying the presence of power and which shifted the bases of this power to fit their organizational and personal relationship with the target office" (Anselm 1980, p. 199).

These observations warrant further investigation. To what extent do mid-level administrators "burrow" into their own offices in response to exclusion from power, not just influence, in institutional policy making? Is the strategy common or one of several? To what extent and in what ways do mid-level administrators actually desire to participate in broad decision making?

Relationship to the organization: Commitment

With all the limitations and frustrations of being a middle manager, especially in colleges and universities, why do people want to do it? Why do they stay?

> *Organizational commitment results (as a dependent variable) from a variety of sociological and psychological circumstances. It also functions as an independent variable and as an intervening variable, producing such behavioral manifestations as unwillingness to leave the organization and the perpetuation of organizational mission* (Thomas 1978, p. 34).

Intrinsic sources rather than extrinsic sources are more strongly related to one's commitment to an organization (Thomas 1978). As responsibility, freedom, and status increase, for example, so too does organizational commitment. Individuals' perceptions of the prestige of their respective positions, of their respective units, and of the university as a whole and their perceptions of their alterna-

---

tives for a career also relate positively to commitment. Perceptions of equity in salary, an extrinsic dimension of work, are unrelated to organizational commitment (Thomas 1978).

The large majority of mid-level administrators in a large public research university indicated that their greatest commitment was to the position they held or to the university where they worked (Austin forthcoming). Only one-fifth cited a career in higher education as their primary commitment, greater than their commitment to the position or to the employing university. This group of career-oriented administrators had been employed at the university significantly fewer years, on the average, than the administrators who were most committed to the university or the position they held.

Such intrinsic factors as the autonomy experienced in work in higher education, the pride in the contributions higher education makes to society, and the opportunity to meet interesting people are especially important reasons for commitment. Salary, an extrinsic factor, is not as strong a contributor to commitment to work as the various intrinsic factors. If, however, administrators perceive that their salary slips too far in comparison to their faculty colleagues or that the university does not sufficiently value their contribution, salary becomes increasingly important (Austin forthcoming).

Much remains to be learned about the sources of academic middle administrators' commitment, the factors detracting from that commitment, and the relationship between commitment and various outcomes. The research to date suggests that mid-level administrators in higher education are committed largely because they believe in and take pride in what they are doing, because they like the autonomy available in their work, and because they like the people with whom they deal. One might speculate, however, on the effect of conditions that diminish administrators' status. As time passes, one might expect the negative aspects of their jobs to detract from their commitment to the institution. The existing data suggest, however, that intrinsic aspects of their work may compensate for the less attractive extrinsic aspects. Institutional commitment may increase with length of employment (Austin forthcoming), but this speculation requires further investigation.

It is important to note that, while intrinsic reasons are very important in contributing to mid-level administrators' commitment, the extrinsic factors should not be neglected. If administrators feel that they are not valued for their contributions and not rewarded to at least some reasonable degree, their commitment may be threatened.

Outcomes of middle administrators' work

Faculty members' scholarly work is evaluated carefully and efforts are made to assess the impact of their teaching, but administrators' work is rarely evaluated systematically. Admissions directors will know whether they have succeeded in bringing in a class of the projected size and quality, and financial aid directors may know that all students' applications have been processed. But how do these officers—and the institutional researchers, registrars, directors of maintenance services, and myriad others— know whether they are doing a good job?

When asked about desirable incentives, some middle administrators suggested a "performance evaluation" to assess "the competence and performance of those who manage" (Scott 1978, p. 27). Only a few institutions and several professional associations, such as the Council for the Advancement and Support of Education, presently offer such evaluation programs (Scott 1978).

Satisfaction is one outcome of administrators' work that researchers have studied to some extent. A number of studies report that administrators are quite satisfied with their jobs (Baldridge et al. 1978; Bess and Lodahl 1969; Scott 1978; Solomon and Tierney 1977). In a study of administrators in 22 four-year liberal arts colleges, for example, administrators indicated high levels of satisfaction, with only 10 percent saying they were not satisfied (Solomon and Tierney 1977). Limited opportunities for advancement, lack of time for scholarly work, leisure, and family activities, and insufficient resources and staff were factors contributing to dissatisfaction. Given the frustrations mid-level administrators experience, it is somewhat surprising that their satisfaction is not lower. Perhaps the intrinsic aspects of their work such as those relating to their commitment to the organization also maintain middle administrators' satisfaction, despite their frustrations.

In sum, the literature suggests that several conflicts are built into the positions of mid-level administrators. Those off campus view them as experts and spokesmen, while those on campus overlook or ignore them. While they sometimes are privy to specialized, pertinent information, institutional policy makers often fail to enlist their direct involvement in decision making. Institutional reward systems do not acknowledge their professionalism. Administrators must simultaneously serve and control, sometimes with insufficient resources and staff. Concern with job security, opportunities for advancement, and professional recognition are areas contributing to frustration with the job.

If one imagines a group of managers whose career potential within their organization is clearly limited, whose roles are relatively ambiguous, who have little opportunity to contribute directly to the organization's multiple missions, who receive lower salaries than their industrial or governmental counterparts, and because of their rapid multiplication within the organization are viewed as a sinister influence by a politically powerful faculty, he may have a fairly accurate description of middle level managers employed within American colleges and universities today (Thomas 1978, p. 16).

Increased "federal, state, and corporate requirements for administrative accountability in academic, financial, and personnel matters" backed by strong sanctions (Scott 1978, p. 2), as well as changing societal expectations of and needs from higher education, heighten concern with efficiency and quality performance in higher education. Middle administrators are essential to the achievement of such outcomes. "If we can provide an environment in which our middle managers are more effective, then we can multiply the effectiveness of the entire organization" (Kay 1974, p. 8).

A Foot in Administration, A Foot in Academics: Academic Deans and Department Chairs

Academic deans and department chairs have not been included in the discussion of mid-level administrators, as they are also faculty members. Their professorial role gives them the status not available to administrators without academic appointments. Nevertheless, some of the pressures they face are like those of other mid-level administrators (see Booth 1982 and Griffiths and McCarty 1980 for a more intensive review and discussion of the deanship).

Only in recent years has the academic deanship been the focus of much research (Kapel 1979). Traditionally, the dean has been a faculty member appointed by the president who is expected to stand between the top administration and the faculty (Gould 1964; Meeth 1971; Okun 1981; Wisniewski 1977). As in industrial settings, where middle managers are links between the top management and lower levels, in higher education deans serve as "linking pins" between central administration and faculty (Henderson and Henderson 1974, p. 217; Katz and Kahn 1978, p. 321; Likert 1961, pp. 113–15; Scott 1978, p. 10). Deans usually have had no special administrative training and have held their posts for a limited period of time, after which they have returned to the faculty (see Moore et al. 1983).

Their power is often rather restricted, as faculty have typically controlled curricular decisions and their own research. A dean is often described as "a mediator, a problem-solver, a consensus-former, a conciliator, but rarely as a decision-maker" (Okun 1981, p. 26, citing Baldridge 1971a and Gould 1964). As deans acquire more control over budgets, hiring, and policy making, conflict between the faculty and deans may increase (Okun 1981). Deans are less satisfied than chief executive officers (Solomon and Tierney 1977); perhaps one explanation for the dissatisfaction may be the intermediary role deans play.

Several studies investigate perceptions of the dean's role among different university constituencies (Dejnozka 1978; Kapel 1979; Scott 1979a). In a national sample used to analyze the role expectations of the deanship of schools of education held by central administrators, deans of education, chairs of education departments, and education faculty, the four groups agreed about the dean's role in external relations, in evaluation of people and programs, and in monitoring programs and people. Overall, however, deans and central administrators felt that deans should act more like line officers than did the faculty and department chairs. Deans identify with top administrators (Dejnozka 1978; Kapel 1979).

While role conflict seems to be built into the dean's position, department chairs also experience it. The title of a recent monograph, *The Department Chair: Professional Development and Role Conflict* (Booth 1982), underlines the pervasiveness of the experience. Of 39 chairs at Pennsylvania State University, all but two indicated that they had not received any charge when assuming the position (Bragg 1980). Consequently, they experienced feelings of conflict and ambiguity. Without realistic priorities or goals, they could not assess their achievement. Without such guidelines, these department chairs focused on whatever activities each did best (Bragg 1980). Another study in seven Florida universities also found role conflict among department chairs: Department chairs experienced "incompatible expectations" from deans, other chairs, and faculty (Carroll 1976, p. 245). Department chairs felt the greatest conflict about such personnel decisions as promotion and salary level, which are increasingly constrained by limited budgets. That these particular areas cause considerable conflict is not surprising, as department chairs are active faculty members as well as administrators. This specific dichotomy is evident in Kapel's study (1979). Some department chairs' answers were like faculty; others answered more like deans and central administrators.

A statistically significant correlation exists between the presence of role conflict with decreased job satisfaction for department chairs (Carroll 1976). This finding is consistent with observations in many organizational settings, which show that role conflict contributes to low job satisfaction, low confidence in the organization, and high job-related tension (Kahn et al. 1964). Tighter budgets are only likely to heighten these problems.

> *The central problem appears to be the growing demands for accountability in departments at the same time that resources for departments are reduced. This changes the character of academic leadership so that "leaders must mediate between an increased number of constituencies both within and outside the academic department, constituencies that press a number of conflicting criteria for decision-making"* (Booth 1982, p. 22, citing Smelser and Content 1980, p. 172).

Though aspects of their responsibilities for personnel and program development are apparently satisfying for some department chairs (McLaughlin, Montgomery, and Malpass 1975), the position clearly involves considerable role conflict. As department chairs make decisions under conditions of economic constraint, this conflict becomes more apparent.

Lower-level Administrators
Many studies have been done on aspects of the work experience of lower-level and entry-level administrators, particularly in student personnel. These studies are usually narrowly focused, however, and generally do not comprehensively describe or analyze the work experience of lower-level administrators. Within the scope of this research report, it has not been possible to review carefully the many individual studies. The work experience of entry-level admissions counselors, financial aid counselors, personnel counselors, resident heads, development officers, institutional research assistants, and other lower-level administrators may be similar in some ways to that of mid-level administrators, but a comprehensive and analytic review of past research and the gaps in it is needed.

Summary
Administrators differ in their hierarchical level and their functional responsibilities. Like faculty, administrators at all levels are being asked to do more with less. Administrators are particularly sensitive to their institutions' dual organizational structure. Deans and department chairs operate in the bureaucracy and the collegium at the same time—and are subject to the pressures of both worlds. Those who work almost exclusively in the bureaucratic structure find that the collegial structure impinges on their work and sense of self, even as the bureaucratic structure is gaining in dominance. While they are moving toward greater professionalization, middle administrators must continue to accept lower status, limited participation in institutional decision making, ambiguous roles, and few opportunities for advancement.

Policy Implications

Retrenchment raises questions that have not yet been explored sufficiently in the literature on work. What approaches will enable the widest participation in the difficult decisions that must be made? How can opportunities for professional growth be improved when budgets are being cut and options for mobility frozen? Perhaps the most important question of all concerns the commitment of those who work in higher education. Under the conditions colleges and universities will be facing in the 1980s and 1990s, how will the generally high commitment of faculty, administrators, and support staff be maintained?

Recent studies of different employee groups show that the intrinsic characteristics of work, satisfaction, and commitment remain quite stable. At the same time, many faculty members and administrators are experiencing a decline in the extrinsic aspects of their work. A general "speed-up"—more work for the same pay—is occurring. Role conflict, stress, and limited time appear to be increasing. For many faculty and administrators, opportunities for mobility are very limited and morale is lower. On many campuses, the physical plant is not maintained to the same standard that it previously was. Though it is open only to speculation, the quality of work life for clerical and support staff is probably also less positive than in years past.

What can be done in this situation? The current literature on effective organizations (Kanter 1983; Naisbitt 1982; Peters and Waterman 1982) leads to the following recommendations: (1) Leaders of colleges and universities must pay more attention to articulating their institutions' purposes; (2) task and decision-making structures must become more collaborative and less hierarchical; (3) persuasive programs for career planning and for the development of all employees must be instituted.

Pay more attention to articulating purposes

Relatively separate structures for administrators and faculty have been accepted over the years. Now, however, a struggle seems to be underway between the bureaucratic and the collegial structures, and the bureaucratic structure seems to be gaining. This gain is not because senior administrators are power-hungry people; many of them are former faculty members (Moore 1983a) who have probably resisted the centralization of power. In fact, many administrators, "from presidents on down, feel almost overwhelmed by demands of the bureaucracy that call for accountability but provide few rewards and give campus leaders little freedom to make their own decisions" (Carnegie Foundation 1982, p. 89). Presidents, deans, and their staffs do not necessarily gain as the bureaucratic structure expands.

The situation is vastly more complicated, more structural. While individual faculty members may continue to find their lives as academics personally satisfying, the academic corporate body has lost its sense of purpose. Splintered by differences among the disciplines in perspective and method and organized into departments, the faculty, particularly in universities, has been unable to act together on anything significant for a long time. This problem was not serious when enrollments were up and research money was plentiful. But as funds have shrunk, the faculty has trapped itself in the discipline-bound structure. Faculty find themselves competing with one another across departments—now, even within departments—for portions of a smaller pie. Individuals or bands of faculty occasionally break out, but they pay a high price in lost time, few rewards, and isolation—as they struggle, along with their colleagues, to teach more courses, write more articles, and serve on more committees.

The shift in power to the administration is more than a matter of "governance." It also affects the "normative orientation" (Etzioni 1961)—the soul—of higher education. "Utilitarian orientations" curdle idealism. This is an especially dangerous situation if the tenured faculty, who will on the whole stay around, turn their wits to "getting theirs." Time servers, apparatchiks, and operators have always been around, but they were exceptions rather than the rule.

Higher education has always run on the commitment of its employees to do more. Commitment is a precious resource, one that turns out to be a key to the productivity and effectiveness of most organizations (Katzell, Yankelovich et al. 1975; Peters and Waterman 1982). Employees' commitment is based on a sense that the institution in which they work is worthy and cares about them. Leaders are crucial in shaping the atmosphere that gives rise to

Task and decision-making structures must become more collaborative and less hierarchical. . . .

these feelings. Indeed, most effective organizations have leaders who constantly articulate their institutions' beliefs. In coping with financial problems, many leaders of colleges and universities have forgotten that the prime activity for managers is to shape the culture of their institutions (Peters and Waterman 1982). These leaders could learn a good deal from colleges of character, which have managed to survive against many odds (Clark 1970; Martin 1982).

Make task and decision-making structures more collaborative
In business and industry, much attention is being directed to Japanese techniques for management (Ouchi 1981). Cultural differences make importation of such techniques into American settings complex and far from automatic. Nevertheless, certain principles seem to apply to the United States. Effective organizational structures are flexible, staffing is rather lean, and communication frequent and direct. Subunits have permeable boundaries, and work groups shift as new needs arise. While their organizational charts may look messy—if they have any at all—and their hierarchies flat, such organizations do their work creatively and efficiently.

Colleges and universities are traditional organizations— and rightly so. The commitment to collegiality, to tenure, to the protection of the cultural heritage have all insulated higher education from the vagaries of the market. It is now known from the literature on effective organizations that it is not tradition, which after all is the basis for the sense of purpose in many colleges and universities, but the centralization of power and the bureaucratization of decision making that threaten higher education, just as they threaten other organizations (Kanter 1983; Naisbitt 1982; Peters and Waterman 1982). For whether they are traditional or nontraditional, effective organizations make the best use of their employees by encouraging collaboration in the pursuit of their goals. People writing about higher education are starting to examine the importance of collaboration in colleges and universities (Nichols 1982; Spiro and Campbell 1983). The participatory approach to management—or a consultive approach to decision making in academe—can lead to consensus and better understanding.

Consultation involves opening decision-making processes to concerned constituencies holding diverse points

of view in the hope that reasoned discourse and patient,
far-ranging discussion may lead to consensus on issues
or to better mutual understanding of the needs, goals,
and interests of each group involved (Powers and
Powers 1983, p. 219).

Consultive decision making involves the participation of
employees at all levels in decisions that affect them. A key
to this participation is full availability of the information
needed to make decisions in a form that employees can
understand and use (Peters and Waterman 1982). A leader
does not abdicate responsibility by using a participatory
approach. Leaders still must make hard decisions, but they
do so by involving as many people as possible in developing ideas, writing and discussing position papers, and
building support for the best decision.

While time is required for people to develop the skills
that contribute to good participatory decision making and a
certain amount of time is also needed for deliberation, the
advantages of consultive decision making outweigh the
disadvantages (Powers and Powers 1983). It generates
many good ideas; because information is gathered widely
and the knowledge and skills of many people are used,
better decisions result. Consultive decision making also
supports people's needs for personal achievement, autonomy, and psychological growth. It often increases the
productivity of faculty, administrators, and staff who
understand how and why a decision is reached. And,
finally, participatory decision making increases the legitimacy of decisions and the trust and understanding of
constituent groups.

These ideas are intriguing, and they are worth pursuing
seriously as they become perfected in other sectors. The
translation of practices suitable for business and industry
into colleges and universities will require great sensitivity
and sophistication. While Powers and Powers (1983) provide a framework for efforts of this kind, specific examples
of successful participatory decision making in higher
education will take some time to develop. Those colleges
and universities where faculty members are collaborating
to improve the undergraduate curriculum provide some
examples from which we can learn (Gaff 1983; Gamson
forthcoming).

These efforts will succeed to the extent that faculty, administrators, and staff members feel that they are full, participating, valued citizens of their institutions. This process will be slow and difficult for the many institutions that have lost—or never had—a community. No simple formulas work under conditions of retrenchment (Jedamus, Peterson, and Associates 1980; Mingle and Associates 1981). One obvious aspect of the problem is that workers in higher education—faculty members in particular—are not rewarded for being "citizens."

Institute career planning and development for all employees

Faculty, even in teaching-oriented institutions, are promoted and given salary increases according to the number of articles and books they publish. While publications may bring luster to scholars in their disciplines and reflected glory (as well as much-coveted overhead monies) to their institutions, they do not help much in the daily life of institutions. Nor do they contribute significantly to the central purpose of most colleges and universities—undergraduate teaching. These schools must stop emulating the research universities, which are more in the business of producing knowledge than of teaching, and rebalance the emphasis on scholarship versus teaching and service. It is only then that faculty will be willing and able to engage in collaborative work and consultive decision making.

Coincident with a focus on the reward structure should be an all-out effort to expand the mobility and choice of the individuals working in higher education. Several researchers have suggested approaches to faculty development, and some of these ideas could be adopted for administrators and staff as well (Schurr 1980; Shulman 1980, 1983; Toombs and Marlier 1981; West 1980). Innovative arrangements of workload might be developed to stimulate faculty members' growth (Shulman 1980). Recommendations include in-house visiting lectureship programs in which professors are selected to serve as resource people to other faculty members and special lecturers for classes other than their own. Professors also could be given short administrative assignments to expand their knowledge and experience. To retrain professors for new areas of teaching, universities and colleges might develop summer or year-long internships in government or industry and exchange programs with other academic and nonacademic institutions (Schurr 1980; Toombs and Marlier 1981). Options include early retirement plans with cash settlements and partial benefits typically awarded only at retirement. Phased retirement, allowing for several years of part-time employment, is another possibility.

The problem of limited mobility must also be faced. Schurr (1980) recommends that foundations or government agencies organize "a concerted program of collecting, refining, developing and disseminating model institutional policies which both involve faculty members in dealing with career constraints and enable faculty members to develop career options" (p. 20). Other ideas include summer workshops at which campus teams could share ideas and develop strategies to deal with problems of mobility, multicampus career planning centers and libraries, and publication programs on career options. Several cooperating institutions or foundations could provide emergency assistance for terminated faculty members (Schurr 1980).

Little has been written about the need to provide career planning and opportunities for growth for administrative and staff members. The rapid diffusion of human resource development programs and quality circles in business and industry is an important source of ideas for higher education (Bowles, Gordon, and Weisskopf 1983; Simmons and Mares 1983; Yankelovich and Immerwahr 1983).

While the results of the recommended efforts cannot be predicted exactly, they are clearly worth undertaking. For it is only now that it is being recognized that the structures that worked in the expansionary period are not working well now. While colleges and universities do not have much control over their external resources, they can generally choose how to distribute their resources internally, according to what principles and which procedures. The response to constraint in the past decade has been to push existing structures and the people in them to their limits and hope for the best. But no one seems to gain from such organizational naïveté. It is time to learn from the best organizational research and practice. If the imagination and resources that are directed to studying other questions were to be turned to colleges and universities as workplaces, we might find that more rational, less costly ways are available to confront economic problems while remaining faithful to the highest ideals of higher education.

Research Agendas

The enormous amount of literature on higher education hardly ever looks at how colleges and universities operate as workplaces or how the questions that are investigated— whether they be planning strategies, governance structures, or curricular change—affect the way employees work. On the other hand, the well-developed literature on worklife in business and industry rarely touches public sector organizations, let alone colleges and universities.

This report has discussed the peculiarities of colleges and universities as a category—the interpenetrating bureaucratic and collegial structures, the strange varieties of organizational politics, the mixtures of centralization and decentralization. Compared to the private sector, wages and salaries in colleges and universities are often lower and opportunities for advancement are more limited. Psychic rewards have, however, been high, and work has been more varied and autonomous than in other kinds of organizations.

These findings may have been framed by a certain historical period. Some evidence already shows that what was thought to be generally true—that faculty, for instance, are motivated primarily by intrinsic rather than extrinsic rewards—may be most characteristic of the expansionary period. To be sure, changes occur slowly and at different rates (if at all) in different kinds of institutions. On this as well as other matters, comparative research is needed. Making use of instruments developed to describe and diagnose the nature of worklife in other settings (Hackman and Oldham 1980; Institute for Social Research 1980; Quinn and Mangione 1970; Quinn and Shepard 1974) as well as instruments already developed (Austin forthcoming; Bowling Green 1980), studies of different employee groups must be done in a variety of colleges and universities. Account should be taken of the differences related to such variables as size, selectivity, and public or private support that have emerged in several studies as important correlates of work attitudes and activities in higher education.

Throughout the text important questions and gaps are noted. (Tables V, VI, and VII in the appendix summarize areas for future research.) Because there is very little research about the work experience of clerical and other support staff, they are not discussed in this monograph. But these employees have skills that can be used in other types of organizations, and they should be studied. What attracts them to the academic environment? They are essential to the smooth daily operation of their workplaces; understanding the nature of their work and the sources of their frustrations and satisfactions is therefore critical. Women, minorities, and part-time employees, who tend to be concentrated in the lower ranks, should be the focus of more research. Interestingly, the literature on industry and business has focused on the work experience of those lower in the hierarchy and less on those in middle and top management. In contrast, the literature on higher education has had a more elite bias, more frequently examining faculty and senior administrators with less attention to lower-level administrators and support staff.

Another area meriting special attention concerns the measurement of productivity in higher education. It is assumed that satisfaction, opportunities for participation, autonomy, power, and mobility increase productivity and quality, but the literature contains enough controversy about this assumption (Berg et al. 1978; Blumberg 1968; Heckscher 1980; Katz and Kahn 1978) that it is worth special attention in colleges and universities, whose products and organizational structures are quite different.

Collective bargaining is not considered in this review, but collective bargaining among university employees may be a reaction to the increasing pressures on higher education. While a substantial body of literature is developing on this topic (Angell and Kelley 1977; Kemerer and Baldridge 1975, 1981; Lee 1978, 1982; Mortimer and McConnell 1978), research should consider particularly the implications of unions for decision-making power, self-perception, and role conflict among administrators, faculty, and staff. The structure of governance of universities and colleges and the peculiar role of professors bring vexing questions as collective bargaining is introduced into higher education.

In addition to further study within colleges and universities, research should also compare higher education with other sectors. While research funds for large comparative studies are limited, secondary analysis of data sets on worklife in other organizations or from national samples is possible, if not always ideal. Comparisons with business or industrial settings or with government or service agencies may highlight the uniqueness of universities and colleges as well as the ways in which they are similar to other workplaces. Do particular groups of university employees—clericals or administrators, for example—experience their work like their counterparts in other organizations, or are they more like other employees in colleges and universities, like the faculty? Comparative study with service and business organizations may provide useful ideas for colleges and universities dealing with retrenchment.

This research agenda has both practical and theoretical implications. Colleges and universities as they function as workplaces are microcosms for investigating basic questions about how organizations and individuals respond to scarcity. In an institutional sector as central as higher education to the fortunes of the nation, this is a critical applied question as well.

APPENDIX

Tables I, II, III, and IV summarize the research on various aspects of the work experience of faculty members, presidents, mid-level administrators, and other administrators, respectively. Each table is divided into sections paralleling the major topical areas of the text. The studies that support the major research findings are also listed.

Tables V, VI, and VII present important issues and questions not yet answered concerning the work experience of faculty, administrators, and support staff, respectively. They too are divided according to the major areas discussed in the text.

TABLE I
SUMMARY OF RECENT RESEARCH ON THE WORK
EXPERIENCE OF FACULTY MEMBERS

Topic	Major Research Findings	Bibliographic Reference
Extrinsic factors in work	*Activities and workload*	
	• Expectations of others are often ambiguous and conflicting.	Blau 1973; Ladd 1979; Rich and Jolicoeur 1978
	• The greatest source of role strain is excessive demands to perform discrete tasks.	Baldwin and Blackburn 1981; Bess 1982; Larkin and Clagett 1981; Wendel 1977
	• Work week averages 44 to 55 hours.	Ladd 1979; Shulman 1980; Wendel 1977
	• The allocation of faculty members' time is related to the type of institution.	Baldridge et al. 1978; Fulton and Trow 1974; Ladd 1979; Rich and Jolicoeur 1978; Shulman 1980; Willie and Stecklein 1981
	• The great majority of faculty prefer teaching, but faculty members are directing increasing attention to research and are publishing more in recent years.	Ladd and Lipsett 1975, 1977; Rich and Jolicoeur 1978; Willie and Stecklein 1981
	Opportunity structure	
	• Limited opportunity for mobility exists within faculty members' own institutions and into other institutions.	Keyfitz 1975; Schurr 1980

Reward structure

	● Financial compensation for faculty is dropping in comparison to cost-of-living increases.	Anderson 1983; Carnegie Council 1980
Intrinsic dimensions in work	● Little empirical study has been performed; only observation and speculation are available to date.	
Power and participation	● Faculty have most influence on academic appointments and least on financial matters.	Baldridge et al. 1973; Kenen and Kenen 1978; Mortimer, Gunne, and Leslie 1976
	● The size, complexity, and prestige of the institution are strongly and positively related to faculty members' autonomy and power.	Baldridge et al. 1973; Blau 1973; Ecker 1973; Kenen and Kenen 1978; Light 1974; Ross 1977; Stonewater 1977
	● Faculty members' rank and credentials are related positively to their influence; status and expertise are the key variables.	Baldridge et al. 1973; Ecker 1973; Kenen and Kenen 1978; Light 1974; Ross 1977
	● Faculty influence at public universities and private nondenominational institutions is greater than at public colleges and denominational institutions.	Cares and Blackburn 1978; Kenen and Kenen 1978
	● Faculty members' participation in governance at institutions of all types has declined sharply over the last decade.	Anderson 1983

Relationship to the organization	• Institutional loyalty is related to faculty members' status in the institution, profession, and discipline. As status in the institution increases, institutional loyalty increases.	Blau 1973; Kenen 1974; Lewis 1967; Nandi 1968; Parsons and Platt 1968; Razak 1969; Spencer 1969
	• Organizational loyalty and professional commitment seem to vary independently.	Razak 1969

Outcomes	*Productivity and performance*	
	• Institutional quality and "colleague climate" are the strongest predictors of productivity as measured by the amount of research.	Behymer 1974; Blau 1973; Finkelstein 1978; Fulton and Trow 1974
	• The relationship between age and research productivity follows a saddle-shaped curve.	Bayer and Dutton 1977; Blackburn, Behymer, and Hall 1978; Fulton and Trow 1974; Pelz and Andrews 1976
	Satisfaction	
	• Satisfaction among faculty is relatively high, though the percentage reporting indifference or dissatisfaction is increasing.	Bennett and Griffitt 1976; Willie and Stecklein 1981
	• Intrinsic factors are more significant than extrinsic factors in explaining job satisfaction. The nature of the work itself, autonomy, relations with others in the institution, and the opportunity to work	Bennett and Griffitt 1976; Bess 1981; Cohen 1973; Willie and Stecklein 1981; Winkler 1982

with students are especially important factors.

- Extrinsic factors—especially salary levels, retirement prospects, time constraints, and lack of equipment, budgetary, and secretarial support—appear to be important determinants of job *dis*satisfaction.

  Bureau of Institutional Research 1974; Clark and Blackburn 1973; Ladd 1979

- Faculty are quite satisfied with the academic career in general, regardless of the type of institution or their age or sex.

  Gaff and Wilson 1975; Willie and Stecklein 1981

Morale

- Faculty morale has been declining over the last decade.

  Anderson 1983

- A major factor contributing to positive morale and satisfaction is involvement in planning and governance.

  Anderson 1983

TABLE II
SUMMARY OF RECENT RESEARCH ON THE WORK
EXPERIENCE OF PRESIDENTS

Topic	Major Research Findings	Bibliographic Reference
Extrinsic factors in work	*Activities and workload*	
	• Many diverse demands are placed on presidents.	Cohen and March 1974
	• Great time pressures are sometimes a source of dissatisfaction.	Buxton, Pritchard, and Buxton 1976; Kauffman 1980
	Opportunity structure	
	• Few opportunities exist for comparable new positions after a presidency.	Cohen and March 1974; Kauffman 1980
	Reward structure	
	• Salary levels for college and university presidents are lower than for comparable positions in business or industry.	Bowen 1978
Intrinsic dimensions in work	• The position of president is intrinsically lonely, although it confers high status on the individual.	Cohen and March 1974; Kauffman 1980; Nason 1980a
	• Expectations are unclear, although the president is under constant scrutiny.	
	• The position confers a high degree of autonomy and power, although current pressures may threaten autonomy, especially in centralized state systems.	
	• The president's power is especially high in establishing budget priorities, long-range planning, personnel policy and	

selection, program development, and decisions concerning the physical plant.

Outcomes

- Satisfaction results from the challenge of the work, decision making, autonomy, relationships with students, faculty, and administrators, and contributions to society.

  Buxton, Pritchard, and Buxton 1976; Kanter 1979; Solomon and Tierney 1977

- Dissatisfaction is associated with external pressures on colleges and universities: economic pressures; limited time; constraints on the authority of presidents in centralized state systems.

  Buxton, Pritchard, and Buxton 1976; Kauffman 1980

TABLE III
**SUMMARY OF RECENT RESEARCH ON THE WORK
EXPERIENCE OF MID-LEVEL ADMINISTRATORS**

Topic	Major Research Findings	Bibliographic Reference
Extrinsic factors in work	*Activities and workload* ● Limited time is a source of frustration.	Scott 1978
	● Actual tasks vary depending on the specific area of administration; in general, the trend is toward increasing specialization.	Anselm 1980; Scott 1978
	Opportunity structure ● Opportunities for upward mobility are limited.	Kanter 1979; Scott 1978, 1979c
	Reward structure ● Salaries are lower than for comparable positions in business or industry.	Scott 1978
Intrinsic dimensions in work	● Tensions are inherent in the relationship between faculty and staff.	Anselm 1980; Baumgartel 1976; Scott 1978; Thomas 1978
	● With the increasing number of mid-level administrators in recent decades, the status for some has dropped.	Scott 1978
Power and participation	● The autonomy to implement decisions may be quite high, but the power to make policy is limited.	Anselm 1980; Kanter 1978; Scott 1978
	● Mid-level administrators have little power to make broad institutional policies but have daily re-	Anselm 1980; Kanter 1978; Scott 1978

	sponsibility to implement policies.	
Relationship to the organization	• Organizational commitment is more strongly related to intrinsic factors than to extrinsic factors; organizational commitment increases as responsibility, freedom, and status increase.	Thomas 1978
Outcomes	• Administrators indicate that they are quite satisfied with their work.	Baldridge et al. 1978; Scott 1978; Solomon and Tierney 1977
	• Dissatisfaction is related to limited opportunities for advancement, limited time, and insufficient resources and staff.	

TABLE IV
SUMMARY OF RECENT RESEARCH ON THE WORK
EXPERIENCE OF OTHER ADMINISTRATORS

Type of Administrator	Major Research Findings	Bibliographic Reference
Deans and department chairs	*Role conflict* • Conflict between deans and faculty increases as deans acquire more control over budgets, hiring, and policy making.	Okun 1981
	• Role conflict is built into the roles of deans and department chairs. The greatest conflict is over such personnel decisions as promotion and salary levels.	Bragg 1980; Carroll 1976
	Satisfactions • Deans and department chairs report less job satisfaction than chief executive officers.	Solomon and Tierney 1977
	• A negative correlation exists between role conflict and job satisfaction for department chairs.	Carroll 1976
Lower-level administrators	• While many studies have been done on specific aspects of the work of lower-level administrators (especially student personnel administrators), few major studies bring together the individual studies.	

TABLE V
DIRECTIONS FOR FUTURE RESEARCH ON THE
WORK EXPERIENCE OF FACULTY MEMBERS

Topic	Issues and Questions
Extrinsic factors in work	*Activities and workload* • How do activities of faculty members in the various disciplines differ? • Faculty workload becomes a sensitive and difficult issue in times of retrenchment. How can workload be allocated to take into account discipline, institutional type, and individual interests? • What new mixtures of responsibilities for teaching and research can be designed that reach beyond traditional disciplinary boundaries? *Opportunity structure* • How can career options and development be expanded for young scholars as well as for senior faculty members? • The specific problems of terminated faculty members have been largely ignored. How can these individuals be assisted? *Reward structure* • Few good models exist to enable cross-institutional comparisons of salary and compensation.
Intrinsic dimensions in work	• The intrinsic dimensions of faculty work are largely unstudied. Empirical research should examine the degree of autonomy, variety, and feedback in faculty members' work. • To what extent is faculty work varied? To what extent is variety diminished in situations where mobility is unlikely? What structural approaches might increase the variety of faculty work despite decreasing options for mobility? • Under the impact of external pressures, are individual faculty members experiencing a decline in their control over their daily work?

- How do faculty members do their scholarly work? Would greater encouragement and reward for collaborative work be one way to increase faculty members' vitality?

Power and participation
- The trend toward centralization of decision making in universities and colleges should be examined. What is the extent of this trend and what are its effects on faculty members?

- Studies link institutional size, complexity, and quality to greater autonomy and power for faculty, but little research analyzes differences in faculty power and participation according to institutional type.

- To what extent and on what issues do faculty members want to participate in decision making? What are the differences between their desire for autonomy over their own work and their desire to participate in decisions of an institutional nature?

- The terms "power," "influence," "autonomy," and "participation" must be more clearly distinguished in the literature and research.

Relationship to the organization

Individual/institutional goal congruence
- How does individual/institutional goal congruence relate to the nature of faculty members' work experience?

- Under what conditions are institutional goal ambiguity and individual/institutional goal conflict most pronounced and destructive?

Loyalty and commitment
- Research has not examined the nature of faculty members' loyalty to their institutions. What promotes and what detracts from the organizational loyalty and commitment of faculty members?

- Under what conditions do faculty members forgo salary and benefit advantages in efforts to help institutions under economic constraint?

Outcomes

Productivity and performance
- Though advances are being made, more research is needed on ways to measure the outcomes of faculty work.
- Studies of the effectiveness of teaching are difficult to compare, because different criteria and measures are used. More work is needed in this area.

Satisfaction
- More research is needed concerning the relationship between faculty members' participation, autonomy, and power and their satisfaction.
- How does institutional stress affect faculty members' satisfaction?

Morale
- What promotes and detracts from faculty members' morale?

TABLE VI
DIRECTIONS FOR FUTURE RESEARCH ON THE
WORK EXPERIENCE OF ADMINISTRATORS

Topic	Issues and Questions
	Presidents/Senior Officers
	• To what extent do college and university presidents feel that their opportunities for mobility are limited? Does a sense of limited options for mobility affect their work?
	• What are the effects of economic pressures and centralized decision making on the way in which presidents feel about their positions? How do such pressures affect their satisfaction? Their level of stress?
	• Vice presidents have not been studied much as a distinct group. While the position may be somewhat similar to the presidency, the dynamics peculiar to that post should be analyzed.
	Deans/Department Chairs
	• Role conflict becomes particularly strong for deans and department chairs when budgets are tight. Further research on the effects of increasing role conflict for these administrators is needed.
	Mid-level Administrators
Extrinsic factors in work	*Activities and workload*
	• What will be the effects of increasing specialization on the ways in which mid-level administrators experience their work?
	Opportunity structure
	• To what extent do mid-level administrators perceive that their options for advancement are limited? How do their perceptions affect their work experience?
	• How can colleges and universities provide opportunities for growth for administrators even when movement to new positions is limited?

Reward structure
- What do mid-level administrators perceive as valuable rewards for their contributions to their institutions?

- How can colleges and universities provide a desirable reward system even in times of retrenchment? How can declining morale and increasing resentment be prevented if salary levels do not keep pace with rewards to other employees?

Intrinsic dimensions in work	• Much remains to be learned about the intrinsic dimensions of administrators' work: variety, professional status, autonomy. • What affects the status of mid-level administrators? How are they perceived by others in their institutions?
Power and participation	• To what extent do mid-level administrators actually desire to participate in broad institutional decision making? • To what extent do mid-level administrators "burrow" into their own offices and responsibilities in response to exclusion from power? • How do middle administrators respond when they are excluded from institutional decision making but must implement such decisions?
Relationship to the organization	• What encourages and what detracts from the commitment of mid-level administrators to their institutions? • What is the relationship between the extent of mid-level administrators' institutional commitment and such outcomes as productivity, performance, and satisfaction?
Outcomes	*Productivity and performance* • Administrators' work rarely is evaluated systematically or regularly. What measures could be used to evaluate the quality of work and productivity of administrators?

Satisfaction
- Further research on those factors that contribute to and detract from administrators' satisfaction would be useful.

Morale
- Despite limitations on mobility and salary levels, particularly in periods of retrenchment, how can institutions build high morale among mid-level administrators?

Lower-level Administrators
- The research on this administrative group is not very extensive. Studies should examine the tasks, work environment, intrinsic and extrinsic work characteristics, and satisfaction of entry- and lower-level administrators.

TABLE VII
DIRECTIONS FOR FUTURE RESEARCH ON THE WORK EXPERIENCE OF SUPPORT AND CLERICAL STAFF

Issues and Questions

- What attracts individuals to the academic environment, even though they have skills that make them very employable in other kinds of organizations?

- To what extent are they committed to their institutions? Why?

- How do the work and the work experience of support and clerical staff in higher education settings differ from those of similar employees in business, government, or service organizations?

REFERENCES

The ERIC Clearinghouse on Higher Education abstracts and indexes the current literature on higher education for the National Institute of Education's monthly bibliographic journal *Resources in Education*. Most of these publications are available through the ERIC Document Reproduction Service (EDRS). For publications cited in this bibliography that are available from EDRS, ordering number and price are included. Readers who wish to order a publication should write to the ERIC Document Reproduction Service, P.O. Box 190, Arlington, Virginia 22210. When ordering, please specify the document number. Documents are available as noted in microfiche (MF) and paper copy (PC). Since prices are subject to change, it is advisable to check the latest issue of *Resources in Education* for current cost based on the number of pages in the publication.

American Association of University Professors. 1983. *The Annual Report on the Economic Status of the Profession, 1982–83*. Washington, D.C.: AAUP.

Anderson, Richard E. 1983. *Higher Education in the 1970s: Preliminary Technical Report for Participating Institutions*. New York: Institute of Higher Education, Teachers College, Columbia University.

Angell, George W., and Kelley, Edward P., Jr. 1977. *Handbook of Faculty Bargaining*. San Francisco: Jossey-Bass.

Anselm, Carol Marie Williams. 1980. "Perceptions of Organization, Power, Status, and Conflict Relative to the Office of Professional Staff in a Complex University." Ph.D. dissertation, University of Michigan.

Astin, Helen S. 1978. "Factors Affecting Women's Scholarly Productivity." In *The Higher Education of Women: Essays in Honor of Rosemary Park*, edited by Helen S. Astin and W. Z. Hirsch. New York: Praeger.

Astin, Helen S., and Bayer, A. E. 1979. "Pervasive Sex Differences in the Academic Reward System: Scholarship, Marriage, and What Else?" In *Academic Rewards in Higher Education*, edited by D. R. Lewis and W. E. Becker, Jr. Cambridge, Mass.: Ballinger.

Astin, Helen S., and Snyder, Mary Beth. July-August 1982. "Affirmative Action 1972–1982: A Decade of Response." *Change* 14: 26–31.

Austin, Ann E. Forthcoming. "Work Orientations of University Mid-level Administrators: Patterns, Antecedents, and Outcomes." Ph.D. dissertation, University of Michigan.

Avakian, A. Nancy. 1971. "An Analysis of Factors Relating to the Job Satisfaction and Dissatisfaction of Faculty Members in

Institutions of Higher Education." Ph.D. dissertation, State
University of New York at Albany.

Baldridge, J. Victor, ed. 1971a. *Academic Governance*. Berkeley:
McCutchan.

———. 1971b. *Power and Conflict in the University: Research in
the Sociology of Complex Organizations*. New York: John
Wiley & Sons.

Baldridge, J. Victor; Curtis, David V.; Ecker, George P.; and
Riley, Gary L. October 1973. "The Impact of Institutional Size
and Complexity on Faculty Autonomy." *Journal of Higher
Education* 44: 532–48.

———. 1978. *Policy Making and Effective Leadership*. San
Francisco: Jossey-Bass.

Baldwin, Roger G., and Blackburn, Robert T. November-
December 1981. "The Academic Career as a Developmental
Process: Implications for Higher Education." *Journal of
Higher Education* 52: 598–614.

Barnard, William W. 1971. "Role Expectations and Role Conflict
in University Faculty Work Activities." Ph.D. dissertation,
University of Michigan.

Barnes, James. 1901. *A Princetonian: A Story of Undergraduate
Life at the College of New Jersey*. New York: G. P. Putnam &
Sons.

Barrett, Thomas C. 1969. *Relationship between Perceived Faculty Participation in the Decision-making Process and Job
Satisfaction in Community Colleges of North Carolina*. Raleigh: North Carolina State University.

Batsche, Catherine N. 1981. *Salary and Compensation in Higher
Education: A Cluster Analytic Approach*. Normal, Ill.: Center
for the Study of Educational Finance and Center for Higher
Education at Illinois State University. ED 202 415. 48 pp. MF–
$1.17; PC not available EDRS.

Baumgartel, Howard. 1976. "Evaluation of Management Development Efforts in the University Setting: Problems, Program-
mers, and Research Model." *New Frontiers in Education*—
Delhi: 23.

Bayer, Alan E., and Dutton, Jeffrey E. May-June 1977. "Career
Age and Research: Professional Activities of Academic Scientists." *Journal of Higher Education* 48: 259–82.

Behymer, Charles E. 1974. "Institutional and Personal Correlates
of Faculty Productivity." Ph.D. dissertation, University of
Michigan.

Benezet, Louis E.; Katz, Joseph; and Magnusson, Francis. 1981.
Style and Substance: Leadership and the College Presidency.
Washington, D.C.: American Council on Education.

Bennett, C. A., and Griffitt, W. B. 1976. *Survey of Faculty Opinion at Kansas State University*. Research Report No. 35. Manhattan, Kan.: Kansas State University Office of Educational Research. ED 160 017. 21 pp. MF–$1.17; PC–$3.74.

Berg, Ivar, et al. 1978. *Managers and Work Reform*. New York: The Free Press.

Bess, James L. 1978. "Incentives for Improving Administrative Competence and Performance." Paper presented to the National Assembly of the American Association of University Administrators, 24 April, Chicago.

———. 1981. "Intrinsic Satisfaction from Academic versus Other Professional Work: A Comparative Analysis." Paper presented at the annual meeting of the Association for the Study of Higher Education, March, Washington, D.C. ED 203 805. 52 pp. MF–$1.17; PC–$7.24.

———. 1982. *University Organization: A Matrix Analysis of the Academic Professions*. New York: Human Sciences Press.

Bess, James L., and Lodahl, Thomas M. Spring 1969. "Career Patterns and Satisfactions in University Middle-Management." *Educational Record* 50 (2): 220–29.

Biglan, Anthony. 1971. "The Relationship of University Department Organization to the Characteristics of Academic Tasks." Ph.D. dissertation, University of Illinois.

Blackburn, Robert T.; Behymer, C. E.; and Hall, D. E. April 1978. "Research Note: Correlates of Faculty Publications." *Sociology of Education* 51:132–41.

Blau, P. M. 1973. *The Organization of Academic Work*. New York: John Wiley & Sons.

Blumberg, Paul. 1968. *Industrial Democracy: The Sociology of Participation*. New York: Schocken Books.

Boland, W. R. 1971. "Size, Organization, and Environmental Mediation: A Study of Colleges and Universities." In *Academic Governance*, edited by J. V. Baldridge. Berkeley: McCutchan.

Booth, David B. 1982. *The Department Chair: Professional Development and Role Conflict*. AAHE-ERIC/Higher Education Research Report No. 10. Washington, D.C.: American Association for Higher Education. ED 226 689. 60 pp. MF–$1.17; PC–$7.24.

Borland, David. 1970. "The University as an Organization: An Analysis of the Faculty Rewards System." Ed.D. dissertation, Indiana University.

Bowen, Howard R. 1978. *Academic Compensation*. New York: Teachers Insurance and Annuity Association. ED 155 994. 139 pp. MF–$1.17; PC–$12.87.

Bowles, Samuel; Gordon, David M.; and Weisskopf, Thomas E.
1983. *Beyond the Waste Land: A Democratic Alternative to
Economic Decline.* New York: Anchor/Doubleday.

Bowling Green State University. 1980. *1980 BGSU Employee
Survey.* Bowling Green, Ohio: Office of Institutional Studies,
Bowling Green State University.

Bragg, Ann Kieffer. 1980. "Relationship between the Role Defini-
tion and Socialization of Academic Department Heads." Ed.D.
dissertation, Pennsylvania State University.

Bucher, Glenn R. 27 April 1981. "Deferring Maintenance on a
College's Faculty." *Chronicle of Higher Education:* 21.

Bureau of Institutional Research. 1974. *University of Illinois
Employees Job Satisfaction Study.* Champaign, Ill.: University
of Illinois, Educational Resources Information Center. ED 132
902. 74 pp. MF–$1.17; PC–$7.24.

Buxton, Thomas H.; Pritchard, Keith W.; and Buxton, Barry M.
Spring 1976. "University Presidents: Academic Chameleons."
Educational Record 57: 79–86.

Cameron, Susan Wilson. 1978. "Women Faculty in Academia:
Sponsorship, Informal Networks, and Scholarly Success."
Ph.D. dissertation, University of Michigan.

Caplow, Theodore, and McGee, Reece J. 1958. *The Academic
Marketplace.* New York: Basic Books.

Carbone, Robert F. 1981. *Presidential Passages.* Washington,
D.C.: American Council on Education.

Cares, Robert C. 1975. "Self-Actualization Attitudes of Faculty
and Their Perceptions of Their Career Success." Ph.D. dissertation, University of Michigan.

Cares, Robert C., and Blackburn, Robert T. October 1978.
"Faculty Self-Actualization: Factors Affecting Career Success." *Research in Higher Education* 9: 123–36.

Carnegie Council on Policy Studies. 1980. *Three Thousand
Futures: The Next Twenty Years for Higher Education.* San
Francisco: Jossey-Bass. ED 183 076. 175 pp. MF–$1.17; PC
not available EDRS.

Carnegie Foundation for the Advancement of Teaching. 1982.
The Control of the Campus. Lawrenceville, N.J.: Princeton
University Press.

Carroll, Archie B. Autumn 1976. "The Role Conflict Phenome-
non: Implications for Department Chairmen and Academic
Faculty." *Improving College and University Teaching* 24:
245–46.

Caston, Geoffrey. 1977. "Conflicts within the University Community." *Studies in Higher Education* 21: 3–8.

Cather, Willa. 1925. *The Professor's House*. New York: Knopf.

Chronicle of Higher Education. 6 October 1982. "New Assistant Professors' Pay Varies as Much as $5,800 at State Colleges": 29.

————. 2 March 1983a. "Fact-File: Median Salaries of Administrators, 1982–83": 26.

————. 9 March 1983b. "Fact-File: Median Salaries for Administrators in Secondary Positions, 1982–83": 23–24.

Clark, Burton R. 1970. *The Distinctive College: Antioch, Reed, and Swarthmore*. Chicago: Aldine.

Clark, Mary Jo. 1973. "A Study of Organizational Stress and Professional Performance of Faculty Members in a Small Four-Year College." Ph.D. dissertation, University of Michigan.

Clark, Mary Jo, and Blackburn, Robert T. 1973. "Faculty Performance under Stress." In *Proceedings: The First Invitational Conference on Faculty Effectiveness as Evaluated by Students*, edited by Alan L. Sockloff. Philadelphia: Measurement and Research Center, Temple University.

Cohen, Arthur M. 1973. *Work Satisfaction among Junior College Faculty Members*. Washington, D.C.: National Institute of Education. ED 081 426. 8 pp. MF–$1.17; PC–$3.74.

Cohen, Michael D., and March, James G. 1974. *Leadership and Ambiguity: The American College President*. New York: McGraw-Hill.

Corson, John J. 1960. *Governance of Colleges and Universities*. New York: McGraw-Hill.

————. 1975. *The Governance of Colleges and Universities: Modernizing Structure and Processes*. Rev. ed. New York: McGraw-Hill.

————. 1979. *Management of the College or University: It's Different!* Topical Paper No. 16. Tucson: Center for the Study of Higher Education, University of Arizona. ED 177 976. 19 pp. MF–$1.17; PC–$3.74.

Dejnozka, Edward L. September-October 1978. "The Dean of Education: A Study of Selected Role Norms." *Journal of Teacher Education* 29: 81–84.

Demerath, N. J.; Stephens, R. W.; and Taylor, R. R. 1967. *Power, Presidents, and Professors*. New York: Basic Books.

DeVries, David L. 1970. "The Relationship of Departmental and Personal Role Expectations to the Role Behaviors of University Faculty Members." Ph.D. dissertation, University of Illinois.

Douglas, Joel M.; Krause, Loren A.; and Winogora, Leonard. 1980. *Workload and Productivity Bargaining in Higher Education*. Monograph No. 3. New York: National Center for the

Study of Collective Bargaining, City University of New York. ED 196 346. 38 pp. MF–$1.17; PC not available EDRS.

Drucker, Peter. 1973. *Management*. New York: Harper & Row.

Ecker, George P. 1973. "Pressure, Structure, and Attitude: Organizational Structure and Faculty Milieux." Doctoral dissertation, Stanford University.

Eckert, Ruth E., and Stecklein, John E. 1961. *Job Motivations and Satisfactions of College Teachers: A Study of Faculty Members in Minnesota Colleges*. Washington, D.C.: U.S. Government Printing Office.

Eckert, Ruth E., and Williams, Howard Y. 1972. *College Faculty View Themselves and Their Jobs*. Minneapolis: College of Education, University of Minnesota. ED 074 960. 64 pp. MF–$1.17; PC–$7.24.

Eckstrom, Ruth B. 1979. "Women Faculty, Development, Promotion, and Pay." *Findings* 5 (2): 1–5.

Edmundson, James C. 1969. *An Identification of Selected Items Associated with Faculty Job Satisfaction in the North Carolina System of Community Colleges*. Raleigh: North Carolina State University.

Elmore, Charles J. 1979. "Black Faculty in White University Arts and Science Departments: Some Environmental Aspects Related to Job Satisfaction." Ph.D. dissertation, University of Michigan.

Etzioni, Amitai. 1961. *A Comparative Analysis of Complex Organizations: On Power, Involvement, and Their Correlates*. 1st ed. New York: Free Press of Glencoe.

Ferguson, John. 1960. "Job Satisfaction and Job Performance within a University Faculty." Ph.D. dissertation, Cornell University.

Finkelstein, Martin J. 1978. "Three Decades of Research on American Academics: A Descriptive Portrait and Synthesis of Findings." Ph.D. dissertation, State University of New York–Buffalo.

Flandrau, Charles M. 1897. *Harvard Episodes*. Freeport, N.Y.: Books for Libraries Press.

Forrest, Aubrey. 1981. *COMP-ACT: Increasing Student Competence and Persistence: The Best Case for General Education*. Iowa City, Iowa: The American College Testing Program.

Frances, Carol, and Mensel, R. Frank. Fall 1981. "Women and Minorities in Administration of Higher Education Institutions: Employment Patterns and Salary Comparisons 1978–79 and an Analysis of Progress toward Affirmative Action Goals 1975–76 to 1978–79." *Journal of College and University Personnel Administrators* 32: 1–77.

French, John R. P., Jr.; Tupper, C. J.; and Mueller, E. F. 1965. "Work Load of University Professors." Unpublished paper, University of Michigan. ED 003 329. 278 pp. MF–$1.17; PC–$23.74.

Fuchs, Rachel G., and Lovano-Kerr, Jessie. 1981. "Retention, Professional Development, and Quality of Life: A Comparative Study of Male/Female Non-Tenured Faculty." Paper presented at the annual meeting of the American Educational Research Association, Los Angeles. ED 202 416. 26 pp. MF–$1.17; PC–$5.49.

Fulton, O., and Trow, M. Winter 1974. "Research Activity in American Higher Education." *Sociology of Education* 47: 29–73.

Furniss, W. Todd, and Graham, Patricia A. 1974. *Women in Higher Education*. Washington, D.C.: American Council on Education.

Gaff, Jerry G. 1983. *General Education Today: A Critical Analysis of Controversies, Practices, and Reforms*. San Francisco: Jossey-Bass.

Gaff, Jerry G., and Wilson, Robert C. 1975. "Faculty Impact on Students." In *College Professors and Their Impact on Students,* edited by Robert C. Wilson, Jerry G. Gaff, Evelyn R. Dienst, Lynn Wood, and James L. Barry. New York: John Wiley & Sons.

Gamson, Zelda F. Forthcoming. *Liberating Education: Liberal Education in the 1980s*. San Francisco: Jossey-Bass.

Gappa, Judith M., and Uehling, Barbara S. 1979. *Women in Academe: Steps to Greater Equality*. AAHE-ERIC/Higher Education Research Report No. 1. Washington, D.C.: American Association for Higher Education. ED 169 873. 97 pp. MF–$1.17; PC–$9.37.

Gould, J. W. 1964. *The Academic Deanship*. New York: Columbia University, Teachers College Press.

Gouldner, Alvin W. December 1957. "Cosmopolitans and Locals: Toward an Analysis of Latent Social Roles." *Administrative Science Quarterly* 2: 281–306.

———. March 1958. "Cosmopolitans and Locals: Toward an Analysis of Latent Social Roles." *Administrative Science Quarterly* 2: 444–80.

Griffiths, Daniel E., and McCarty, Donald J. 1980. *The Dilemma of the Deanship*. Danville, Ill.: Interstate Printers and Publishers.

Gustad, John W. 1960. *The Career Decisions of College Teachers*. Washington, D.C.: U.S. Department of Health, Education and Welfare.

Haak, Harold H. 1982. *Parable of a President*. Washington,
D.C.: American Association of State Colleges and Universities. ED 225 443. 75 pp. MF–$1.17; PC not available EDRS.

Hackman, J. Richard, and Oldham, Greg R. 1980. *Work Rede-
sign*. Reading, Mass.: Addison-Wesley.

Harrison, Marjorie R. 1981. "The Role of a Professional Head of
Residence: A Comparison of Perceptions." Ed.D. dissertation,
University of Massachusetts.

Harry, Joseph, and Goldner, Norman S. Winter 1972. "The Null
Relationship between Teaching and Research." *Sociology of
Education* 45(1): 47–60.

Hauser, Jane, and Lazarsfeld, Paul. 1964. *The Admissions Officer
in the American College: An Occupation under Change*. New
York: College Entrance Examination Board.

Heckscher, Charles. January-March 1980. "Worker Participation
and Management Control." *Journal of Social Reconstruction*
1: 77–101.

Henderson, Algo, and Henderson, Jean G. 1974. *Higher Education in America: Problems, Priorities, Prospects*. San Francisco: Jossey-Bass.

Herman, Joyce; McArt, Ebba; and Belle, Lawrence. Spring
1983. "New Beginnings: A Study of Faculty Career Changes."
Improving College and University Teaching 31: 53–60.

Herzberg, Frederick. 1973. *Work and the Nature of Man*. Rev.
ed. Cleveland: World Publishing Company.

Hill, Winston W. 1965. "Some Organizational Correlates of
Sanctions Perceived by Professors to Be Available to Their
Departmental Chairman." D.B.A. dissertation, University of
Washington.

Hind, Robert R. 1969. "Evaluation and Authority in a University
Faculty." Ph.D. dissertation, Stanford University.

Hollon, Charles J., and Gemmill, Gary R. Winter 1976. "A
Comparison of Female and Male Professors on Participation in
Decision Making, Job Related Tension, Job Involvement, and
Job Satisfaction." *Educational Administration Quarterly* 12:
80–93.

Hornig, Lilli S. March 1980. "Untenured and Tenuous: The
Status of Women Faculty in Academe." *Annals of the American Academy of Political and Social Science* 448: 115–25.

Hoskins, Robert L. 1978. *Black Administrators in Higher Education*. New York: Praeger Publishers.

Howard, Suzanne. 1978. *But We Will Persist: A Comparative
Research Report on the Status of Women in Academe*. Washington, D.C.: American Association of University Women. ED
179 121. 93 pp. MF–$1.17; PC not available EDRS.

Hunter, Mary; Ventimiglia, Joe; and Crow, Mary Lynn. March-April 1980. "Faculty Morale in Higher Education." *Journal of Teacher Education* 31: 27–30.

Ingraham, Mark H., and King, Francis P. 1968. *The Mirror of Brass: The Compensation and Working Conditions of College and University Administrators*. Madison: University of Wisconsin Press.

Institute for Social Research, The University of Michigan, and Rensis Likert Associates, Inc. 1980. *Survey of Organizations*. Ann Arbor: Institute for Social Research.

Jacobson, Robert L. 27 July 1983. "Faculty Pay Found Higher at Public Colleges than at Private Colleges, but Not in All Fields." *Chronicle of Higher Education*.

Jedamus, Paul; Peterson, Marvin W.; and Associates, eds. 1980. *Improving Academic Management: A Handbook of Planning and Institutional Research*. San Francisco: Jossey-Bass.

Jencks, Christopher, and Riesman, David. 1968. *The Academic Revolution*. Garden City, N.Y.: Anchor/Doubleday.

Johnson, Roosevelt. 1974. *Black Scholars on Higher Education in the 70s*. Columbus, Ohio: ECCA Publications.

Jones, Phillip E. 1977. "The Changing Profile of Black Administrators in Predominately White Colleges and Universities." Paper presented at the Second Annual Conference on Blacks in Higher Education, 14 March, Washington, D.C. ED 138 192. 13 pp. MF–$1.17; PC–$3.74.

Julius, Daniel J. 1977. *Collective Bargaining in Higher Education: The First Decade*. Washington, D.C.: AAHE-ERIC/ Higher Education Research Currents. ED 145 762. 5 pp. MF–$1.17; PC–$3.74.

Kahn, Robert L., et al. 1964. *Organizational Stress*. New York: John Wiley & Sons.

Kanter, Rosabeth. 1977. *Men and Women of the Corporation*. New York: Basic Books.

———. 1978. "The Changing Shape of Work: Psychosocial Trends in America." Current Issues in Higher Education. Washington, D.C.: American Association for Higher Education. ED 193 992. 19 pp. MF–$1.17; PC not available EDRS.

———. 1979. "Changing the Shape of Work: Reform in Academe." In *Perspectives on Leadership*. Current Issues in Higher Education No. 1. Washington, D.C.: American Association for Higher Education. ED 193 997. 26 pp. MF–$1.17; PC not available EDRS.

———. Summer 1981. "Career Growth and Organizational Power: Issues for Educational Management in the 1980's." *Teachers College Record* 82 (4): 553–66.

————. 1983. *The Change Masters: Innovation for Productivity in the American Corporation.* New York: Simon & Schuster.

Kapel, David E. 1979. "The Education Deanship: A Further Analysis." *Research in Higher Education* 10: 99–112.

Katz, Daniel, and Kahn, Robert L. 1978. *The Social Psychology of Organizations.* New York: John Wiley & Sons.

Katzell, Raymond A., and Yankelovich, Daniel, et al. 1975. *Work, Productivity, and Job Satisfaction: An Evaluation of Policy-Related Research.* New York: Harcourt, Brace, Jovanovich.

Kauffman, Joseph F. 1980. *At the Pleasure of the Board: The Service of the College and University President.* Washington, D.C.: American Council on Education.

Kay, Emmanuel. 1974. *The Crisis in Middle Management.* New York: American Management Association.

Kemerer, Frank R., and Baldridge, J. Victor. 1975. *Unions on Campus.* San Francisco: Jossey-Bass.

————. 1981. *Assessing the Impact of Faculty Collective Bargaining.* AAHE-ERIC/Higher Education Research Report No. 8. Washington, D.C.: American Association for Higher Education. ED 216 653. 66 pp. MF–$1.17; PC–$7.24.

Kenen, Peter B., and Kenen, Regina H. April 1978. "Who Thinks Who's in Charge Here: Faculty Perceptions of Influence and Power in the University." *Sociology of Education* 51: 113–23.

Kenen, Regina H. 1974. "Professors' Academic Role Behavior and Attitudes, as Influenced by the Structural Effects and Community Context of the College or University." Ph.D. dissertation, Columbia University.

Kerr, Clark. 1963. *The Uses of the University.* New York: Harper & Row.

Keyfitz, Nathan. 1975. "Organizational Processes in Education." Preliminary minutes of a conference supported by the National Institute of Education, 26 April, Cambridge, Massachusetts. ED 140 726. 34 pp. MF–$1.17; PC not available EDRS.

Kilson, M. 1976. "The Status of Women in Higher Education." *Signs: Journal of Women in Culture and Society* 1 (2): 935–42.

Klapper, Hope L. 1967. "The College Teacher: A Study of Role Performance, Role Preference, and Role Strain." Ph.D. dissertation, Columbia University.

Kohn, Melvin L. July 1976. "Occupational Structure and Alienation." *American Journal of Sociology* 82: 111–30.

Ladd, Everett Carll, Jr. 1979. "The Work Experience of American College Professors: Some Data and an Argument." In *Faculty Career Development.* Current Issues in Higher Education No. 2. Washington, D.C.: American Association for

Higher Education. ED 193 998. 44 pp. MF–$1.17; PC not available EDRS.

Ladd, Everett C., and Lipset, Seymour M. 1975. *Technical Report: 1975 Survey of the American Professoriate*. Storrs, Conn.: Social Science Data Center, University of Connecticut.

———. 1976. *Survey of the Social, Political, and Educational Perspectives of American College and University Faculty: Final Report*. Storrs, Conn.: University of Connecticut. ED 135 278. 427 pp. MF–$1.17; PC–$35.80.

———. 1977. *Survey of the American Professoriate*. Storrs, Conn.: Social Science Data Center, University of Connecticut.

Larkin, Paul, and Clagett, Craig. 1981. *Sources of Faculty Stress and Strategies for Its Management*. Largo, Md.: Office of Institutional Research, Prince Georges Community College. ED 201 250. 19 pp. MF–$1.17; PC–$3.74.

Lazarsfeld, Paul F., and Thielens, Wagner, Jr. 1958. *The Academic Mind: Social Scientists in a Time of Crisis*. Glenco, Ill.: The Free Press.

Lee, Barbara. 1978. *Collective Bargaining in Four-Year Colleges*. Washington, D.C.: American Association for Higher Education. ED 162 542. 85 pp. MF–$1.17; PC–$9.37.

———. Winter 1982. "Contractually Protected Governance Systems at Unionized Colleges." *The Review of Higher Education* 5: 69–85.

Leon, Julio. 1973. "An Investigation of the Applicability of the Two-Factor Theory of Job Satisfaction among College and University Professors." Ph.D. dissertation, University of Arkansas.

Lewis, Darrell R., and Becker, William E., Jr., eds. 1979. *Academic Rewards in Higher Education*. Cambridge, Mass.: Ballinger.

Lewis, Lionel. March 1967. "On Prestige and Loyalty of University Faculty." *Administrative Science Quarterly* 9: 627–42.

Lewis, Lionel S., and Ryan, Michael N. 1977. "The American Professoriate and the Movement toward Unionization." *Higher Education* 6: 139–64.

Light, Donald, Jr. 1974. "Introduction: The Structure of the Academic Professions." *Sociology of Education* 47 (1): 2–28.

Likert, Rensis. 1961. *New Patterns of Management*. New York: McGraw-Hill.

Litwin, James L. 1982. " 'Quality of Work Life' Issues for the University Employee." Paper presented at the annual forum of the Association for Institutional Research, Denver.

Loring, Frederick W. 1871. *Two College Friends*. Boston: Loring Publishers.

McConnell, Thomas R., and Mortimer, Kenneth P. 1971. *The Faculty in University Governance*. Berkeley: Center for Research and Development in Higher Education, University of California. ED 050 703. 206 pp. MF–$1.17; PC–$18.51.

McKeachie, Wilbert J. 1979. "Perspectives from Psychology: Financial Incentives Are Ineffective for Faculty." In *Academic Rewards in Higher Education,* edited by Darrell R. Lewis and William E. Becker, Jr. Cambridge, Mass.: Ballinger.

———. 1983. "Older Faculty Members: Facts and Prescriptions." *AAHE Bulletin* 36(3): 8–10.

McLaughlin, Gerald W.; Montgomery, James R.; and Mahan, B.T. 1979. "Pay, Rank, and Growing Old with More of Each." *Research in Higher Education* 11(1): 23–35.

McLaughlin, Gerald W.; Montgomery, James R.; and Malpass, Leslie F. 1975. "Selected Characteristics, Roles, Goals, and Satisfactions of Department Chairmen in State and Land-Grant Institutions." *Research in Higher Education* 3: 243–59.

Magarrell, Jack. 15 June 1981. "Faculty Salaries Up." *Chronicle of Higher Education:* 1.

———. 20 October 1982a. "Recession Hits State Support for College." *Chronicle of Higher Education:* 1.

———. 10 November 1982b. "Decline in Faculty Morale Laid to Governance Role, Not Salary." *Chronicle of Higher Education:* 1.

Marsh, Herbert W., and Dillon, Kristine E. September-October 1980. "Academic Productivity and Faculty Supplemental Income." *Journal of Higher Education* 51: 546–55.

Marshall, Joan L. 1979. "The Effects of Collective Bargaining on Faculty Salaries in Higher Education." *Journal of Higher Education* 50: 310–22.

Marshall, R. Steven. 1976. "Faculty Views of the University's Organizational Legitimacy: A Case Study." ED 139 353. 23 pp. MF–$1.17; PC not available EDRS.

Martin, Warren Bryan. 1982. *A College of Character: Renewing the Purpose and Content of College Education*. San Francisco: Jossey-Bass.

Meeth, L. R. 1971. "Administration and Leadership." In *Power and Authority: Transformation of Campus Governance,* edited by H. L. Hodgkinson and L. R. Meeth. San Francisco: Jossey-Bass.

Millett, John D. 1962. *The Academic Community*. New York: McGraw-Hill.

Mingle, James R., and Associates. 1981. *Challenges of Retrenchment*. San Francisco: Jossey-Bass.

Monson, Charles H., Jr. Winter 1967. "Metaphors for the University." *Educational Record* 48(1): 20–29.

Moore, Kathryn M. May 1983a. "Examining the Myths of Administrative Careers." *AAHE Bulletin* 35: 3–6.

———. 1983b. "The Top-Line: A Report on Presidents', Provosts', and Deans' Careers." Leaders in Transition Project. Report No. 83-711. University Park, Pa.: Center for the Study of Higher Education, Pennsylvania State University. ED 231 301. 102 pp. MF–$1.17; PC–$11.12.

———. 1983c. *Women and Minorities: Leaders in Transition—A National Study of Higher Education Administrators.* Report No. 83-310. University Park, Pa.: Center for the Study of Higher Education, Pennsylvania State University. ED 225 459. 64 pp. MF–$1.17; PC–$7.24.

Moore, Kathryn; Salimbene, Ann M.; Marlier, Joyce D.; and Bragg, Stephen M. September-October 1983. "The Structure of Presidents' and Deans' Careers." *Journal of Higher Education* 54(5): 500–16.

Moore, Kathryn M., and Wollitzer, Peter A. 1979. *Women in Higher Education: A Comtemporary Bibliography.* Washington, D.C.: National Association of Women Deans, Administrators, and Counselors. ED 175 320. 119 pp. MF–$1.17; PC–$11.12.

Morgan, Richard H. 1970. "The Conflict between Teaching and Research in the Academic Role." Ph.D. dissertation, Columbia University.

Mortimer, Kenneth P.; Gunne, Manual G.; and Leslie, David W. 1976. "Perceived Legitimacy of Decision Making and Academic Governance Patterns in Higher Education: A Comparative Analysis." *Research in Higher Education* 4(3): 273–90.

Mortimer, Kenneth P., and McConnell, T. R. 1978. *Sharing Authority Effectively.* San Francisco: Jossey-Bass.

Mortimer, Kenneth P., and Tierney, Michael L. 1979. *The Three "R's" of the Eighties: Reduction, Reallocation, and Retrenchment.* AAHE-ERIC/Higher Education Research Report No. 4. Washington, D.C.: American Association for Higher Education. ED 172 642. 93 pp. MF–$1.17; PC–$9.37.

Morton, R. K. Summer 1965. "Teacher's Job Load." *Improving College and University Teaching* 12: 155–56.

Naisbitt, John. 1982. *Megatrends: Ten New Directions Transforming Our Lives.* New York: Warner Books.

Nandi, Roshanta. 1968. "Career and Life Organization of Professionals: A Study of Contrasts between College and University Professors." Ph.D. dissertation, University of Minnesota.

Nason, John W. 1980a. *Presidential Search: A Guide to the Process of Selecting and Appointing College and University Presidents*. Washington, D.C.: Association of Governing Boards of Universities and Colleges.

———. 1980b. "Responsibilities of the Governing Board." In *Handbook of College and University Trusteeship*, edited by Richard T. Ingram and Associates. San Francisco: Jossey-Bass.

———. 1980c. "Selecting the Chief Executive." In *Handbook of College and University Trusteeship*, edited by Richard T. Ingram and Associates. San Francisco: Jossey-Bass.

National Center for Education Statistics. 1980. *The Condition of Education*. Washington, D.C.: NCES. ED 188 304. 351 pp. MF–$1.17; PC not available EDRS.

Nichols, D. A. 1 September 1982. "Can 'Theory Z' Be Applied to Academic Management?" *Chronicle of Higher Education:* 72.

Okun, Kathy Anne. 1981. "Deans' Perceptions of Their Ability to Promote Change in Schools of Education." Ph.D. dissertation, University of Michigan.

Ouchi, W. G. 1981. *Theory Z*. Reading, Mass.: Addison-Wesley.

Parelius, Robert James. 1981. "The Troubles with Teaching Undergraduates: Problems Arising from Organizational, Professional, Collegial, and Client Relationships." Paper presented at the annual meeting of the Society for the Study of Social Problems, August, Toronto, Ontario, Canada. ED 210 985. 22 pp. MF–$1.17; PC–$3.74.

Parsons, Talcott, and Platt, Gerald M. 1968. *The Academic Profession: A Pilot Study*. Washington, D.C.: National Science Foundation.

Peck, Robert P. Winter 1983. "The Entrepreneurial College Presidency." *Educational Record* 64: 18–25.

Pelz, Donald C., and Andrews, Frank M. 1976. *Scientists in Organizations*. Rev. ed. New York: John Wiley & Sons.

Peters, D. S. 1974. *And Pleasantly Ignore My Sex: Academic Women, 1974*. Ann Arbor, Mich.: Center for the Study of Higher Education.

Peters, Thomas J., and Waterman, Robert H., Jr. 1982. *In Search of Excellence: Lessons from America's Best-Run Companies*. New York: Harper & Row.

Platt, Gerald M., and Parsons, Talcott. 1970. "Decision-Making in the Academic System: Influence and Power Exchange." In *The State of the University: Authority and Change*, edited by C. E. Kruytbosch. Beverly Hills, Cal.: Sage.

Powers, David R., and Powers, Mary F. 1983. *Making Participatory Management Work*. San Francisco: Jossey-Bass.

Quinn, Robert P., and Mangione, Thomas W. 1970. *The 1969–70 Survey of Working Conditions*. Ann Arbor, Mich.: Institute for Social Research.

Quinn, Robert P., and Shepard, Linda J. 1974. *The 1972–73 Quality of Employment Survey*. Ann Arbor, Mich.: Institute for Social Research.

Razak, Warren N. 1969. "Departmental Structure and Faculty Loyalty in a Major University." Ph.D. dissertation, University of Kansas.

Rice, Eugene. 1980. "Recent Research on Adults and Careers: Implications for Equity, Planning, and Renewal." Paper commissioned by the National Institute on Education. Stockton, Cal.: University of the Pacific.

Rich, Harvey E., and Jolicoeur, Pamela M. 1978. "Faculty Role Perceptions and Preferences in the Seventies." *Sociology of Work and Occupations* 5(4): 423–45.

Roe, Anne. May 1972. "Patterns in Productivity of Scientists." *Science* 176: 940–41.

Ross, R. Danforth. 1977. "Faculty Qualifications and Collegiality: The Role of Influence in University Decision Making." *Research in Higher Education* 6(3): 201–14.

Rossi, Alice S., and Calderwood, Ann. 1973. *Academic Women on the Move*. New York: Russell Sage Foundation.

Sammartino, Peters. 1982. *The President of a Small College*. New York: Cornwall Books.

Schurr, George M. 1980. *Freeing the "Stuck" and Aiding the Terminated: Expanding the Career Horizons of Tenured College Professors*. Dover, Del.: Center for the Study of Values, University of Delaware. ED 195 197. 91 pp. MF–$1.17; PC not available EDRS.

Scott, Robert A. January 1976a. "Do Admissions Counselors Read?" *NACAC Journal* 20: 22–27.

———. Spring 1976b. "The Terms and Tasks of 'Open Admissions.' " *College and University* 51: 287–90.

———. 1978. *Lords, Squires, and Yeomen: Collegiate Middle-Managers and Their Organizations*. AAHE-ERIC/Higher Education Research Report No. 7. Washington, D.C.: American Association for Higher Education. ED 165 641. 83 pp. MF–$1.17; PC–$9.37.

———. Winter 1979a. "The 'Amateur' Dean in a Complex University: An Essay on Role Ambiguity." *Liberal Education* 65: 445–53.

————. Winter 1979b. "Beleaguered Yeomen: Comments on the Condition of Collegiate Middle-Managers." *College and University* 54: 89–95.

————. 1979c. "Robots or Reinsmen: Job Opportunities and Professional Standing for Collegiate Administrators in the 1980s." Current Issues in Higher Education No 7. Washington, D.C.: American Association for Higher Education. ED 194 003. 28 pp. MF–$1.17; PC not available EDRS.

Scott, W. R. 1966. "Professionals in Bureaucracies: Areas of Conflict." In *Professionalization,* edited by H. M. Vollmer and D. L. Mills. Englewood Cliffs, N.J.: Prentice-Hall.

Setoodeh, Hassan. 1981. "A Study of Position of the Chief Financial Officer in Higher Education Institutions." Ph.D. dissertation, North Texas State University.

Shulman, Carol Herrnstadt. October 1980. "Do Faculty Really Work That Hard?" AAHE-ERIC/Higher Education Research Currents. Washington, D.C.: American Association for Higher Education. ED 192 668. 5 pp. MF–$1.17; PC–$3.74.

————. November 1983. "Fifteen Years Down, Twenty-Five to Go: A Look at Faculty Careers." *AAHE Bulletin* 36(3): 11–14.

Simmons, John, and Mares, William. 1983. *Working Together.* New York: Alfred A. Knopf.

Smart, John C. September-October 1978. "Diversity of Academic Organizations: Faculty Incentives." *Journal of Higher Education* 49: 403–19.

Smelser, Neil J., and Content, Robin. 1980. *The Changing Academic Market.* Berkeley: University of California Press.

Solomon, Lewis C., and Tierney, Michael L. July-August 1977. "Determinants of Job Satisfaction among College Administrators." *Journal of Higher Education* 48: 412–31.

Spencer, Douglas D. 1969. "The Career and Professional Orientations of Non-Doctorate Faculty Members in State Colleges." Ph.D. dissertation, University of Michigan.

Spiro, Louis M., and Campbell, Jill F. 1983. "Higher Education and Japanese Management: Are They Compatible?" Paper presented at the annual forum of the Association for Institutional Research, May, Toronto. ED 232 578. 24 pp. MF–$1.17; PC–$3.74.

Stonewater, Barbara Bradley. 1977. "Faculty and Administrator Perceptions of Power and Influence in University Decision-Making." Ph.D. dissertation, Michigan State University.

Suinn, Richard M., and Witt, Joseph C. November 1982. "Survey on Ethnic Minority Faculty Recruitment and Retention." *American Psychologist* 37(11): 1239–44.

Swierenga, Lloyd G. 1970. "Application of Herzberg's Dual-Factor Theory to FacultyMembers in a University." Ed.D. dissertation, Western Michigan University.

Theophilus, Donald K. 1967. "Professorial Attitudes toward Their Work Environment: A Study of Selected Incentives." Ph.D. dissertation, University of Michigan.

Thomas, Gerald S. 1978. "Organizational Commitment: Sources and Implications for the Development of Middle Managers." Ph.D. dissertation, Cornell University.

Thompson, R. K. 1971. "How Does the Faculty Spend Its Time?" Mimeographed. Seattle: University of Washington.

Toombs, William, and Marlier, Joyce. 1981. "Career Changes among Academics: Dimensions of Decision." Paper presented at the annual meeting of the American Educational Research Association, April, Los Angeles. ED 202 423. 40 pp. MF–$1.17; PC–$5.49.

Touraine, Alan. 1974. *The Academic System in American Society*. New York: McGraw-Hill.

Tuckman, Howard P. December 1978. "Who Is Part-Time in Academe?" *AAUP Bulletin* 64: 305–15.

University of Maryland. 1981. *The Post–Land Grant University: The University of Maryland Report*. Delphi, Md.: University of Maryland System.

Van Alstyne, C.; Mensel, R. F.; Withers, J. S.; and Malott, F. S. 1977. *1975–76 Administrative Compensation Survey: Women and Minorities in Administration of Higher Education Institutions*. Washington, D.C.: College and University Personnel Association.

Vinson, David D. 1977. "The Admissions Officer: A Decade of Change." Ph.D. dissertation, University of Wisconsin.

Weick, Karl E. March 1976. "Educational Organizations as Loosely Coupled Systems." *Administrative Science Quarterly* 21: 1–19.

Wendel, Frederick C. Spring 1977. "The Faculty Member's Work Load." *Improving College and University Teaching* 25: 82.

West, David A. 1980. "Faculty Morale and Career Choice in the 1980s." ED 192 703. 6 pp. MF–$1.17; PC–$3.74.

Wheeless, Virginia E., and Howard, Richard D. 1983. "An Examination of the Non-Faculty University as a Human Resource." Paper presented at the annual forum of the Association for Institutional Research, Toronto. ED 232 559. 27 pp. MF–$1.17; PC–$5.49.

Whitla, Dean K. 1977. *Value Added: Measuring the Outcomes of Undergraduate Education*. Cambridge, Mass.: Office of Instructional Research and Evaluation, Harvard University.

Whitlock, Gerald H. 1965. "The Experiential Bases and Dimensions of Faculty Morale at a State University." Mimeographed. Knoxville, Tenn.: University of Tennessee.

Willie, Reynold, and Stecklein, John E. 1981. "A Three-Decade Comparison of College Faculty Characteristics, Satisfactions, Activities, and Attitudes." Paper presented at the annual forum of the Association for Institutional Research, Minneapolis, Minnesota. ED 205 113. 25 pp. MF–$1.17; PC–$3.74.

Wilson, Logan. 1964. *The Academic Man: A Study in the Sociology of a Profession.* 2d ed. New York: Octagon Books.

Wilson, R. C.; Woods, L.; and Gaff, J. G. 1974. "Social-Psychological Accessibility and Faculty-Student Interaction beyond the Classroom." *Sociology of Education* 47(1): 74–92.

Winkler, Larry Dean. 1982. "Job Satisfaction of University Faculty in the U.S." Ph.D. dissertation, University of Nebraska–Lincoln.

Winter, David G.; McClelland, David C.; and Stewart, Abigail J. 1981. *A New Case for the Liberal Arts.* San Francisco: Jossey-Bass.

Wisniewski, R. 1977. "The Dean of Education and the Looking-Glass Self." Paper presented at the annual meeting of the Society of Professors of Education, March, Chicago, Illinois. ED 162 443. 23 pp. MF–$1.17; PC–$3.74.

Wittenauer, Martha Anne. 1980. "Job Satisfaction and Faculty Motivation." Ed.D. dissertation, Indiana University.

Yankelovich, Daniel, and Immerwahr, John. 1983. *Putting the Work Ethic to Work: A Public Agenda Report on Restoring America's Competitive Vitality.* New York: The Public Agenda Foundation.

Yuker, Harold E. 1974. *Faculty Workload: Facts, Myths, and Commentary.* AAHE-ERIC/Higher Education Research Report No. 6. Washington, D.C.: American Association for Higher Education. ED 095 756. 70 pp. MF–$1.17; PC–$7.24.

ASHE-ERIC HIGHER EDUCATION
RESEARCH REPORTS

Starting in 1983, the Association for the Study of Higher Education assumed co-sponsorship of the Higher Education Research Reports with the ERIC Clearinghouse on Higher Education. For the previous 11 years, ERIC and the American Association for Higher Education prepared and published the reports.

Each report is the definitive analysis of a tough higher education problem, based on a thorough research of pertinent literature and institutional experiences. Report topics, identified by a national survey, are written by noted practitioners and scholars with prepublication manuscript reviews by experts.

Ten monographs in the ASHE-ERIC Higher Education Research Report series are published each year, available individually or by subscription. Subscription to 10 issues is $50 regular; $35 for members of AERA, AAHE, and AIR; $30 for members of ASHE. (Add $7.50 outside U.S.)

Prices for single copies, including 4th class postage and handling, are $6.50 regular and $5.00 for members of AERA, AAHE, AIR, and ASHE. If faster first-class postage is desired for U.S. and Canadian orders, for each publication ordered add $.60; for overseas, add $4.50. For VISA and MasterCard payments, give card number, expiration date, and signature. Orders under $25 must be prepaid. Bulk discounts are available on orders of 10 or more of a single title. Order from the Publications Department, Association for the Study of Higher Education, One Dupont Circle, Suite 630, Washington, D.C. 20036, (202) 296-2597. Write for a complete list of Higher Education Research Reports and other ASHE and ERIC publications.

1981 Higher Education Research Reports

1. Minority Access to Higher Education
   Jean L. Preer

2. Institutional Advancement Strategies in Hard Times
   Michael D. Richards and Gerald Sherratt

3. Functional Literacy in the College Setting
   Richard C. Richardson, Jr., Kathryn J. Martens, and Elizabeth C. Fisk

4. Indices of Quality in the Undergraduate Experience
   George D. Kuh

5. Marketing in Higher Education
   Stanley M. Grabowski

6. Computer Literacy in Higher Education
   Francis E. Masat

7. Financial Analysis for Academic Units
   Donald L. Walters

8. Assessing the Impact of Faculty Collective Bargaining
   J. Victor Baldridge, Frank R. Kemerer, and Associates

9. Strategic Planning, Management, and Decision Making
   Robert G. Cope

10. Organizational Communication in Higher Education
    Robert D. Gratz and Philip J. Salem

1982 Higher Education Research Reports

1. Rating College Teaching: Criterion Studies of Student
   Evaluation-of-Instruction Instruments
   Sidney E. Benton

2. Faculty Evaluation: The Use of Explicit Criteria for
   Promotion, Retention, and Tenure
   Neal Whitman and Elaine Weiss

3. The Enrollment Crisis: Factors, Actors, and Impacts
   *J. Victor Baldridge, Frank R. Kemerer, and Kenneth C.
   Green*

4. Improving Instruction: Issues and Alternatives for Higher
   Education
   Charles C. Cole, Jr.

5. Planning for Program Discontinuance: From Default to
   Design
   Gerlinda S. Melchiori

6. State Planning, Budgeting, and Accountability: Approaches
   for Higher Education
   Carol E. Floyd

7. The Process of Change in Higher Education Institutions
   Robert C. Nordvall

8. Information Systems and Technological Decisions: A Guide
   for Non-Technical Administrators
   Robert L. Bailey

9. Government Support for Minority Participation in Higher
   Education
   Kenneth C. Green

10. The Department Chair: Professional Development and Role
    Conflict
    David B. Booth

1983 Higher Education Research Reports

1. The Path to Excellence: Quality Assurance in Higher
   Education
   *Laurence R. Marcus, Anita O. Leone, and Edward D.
   Goldberg*

INDEX

1983
ASHE-ERIC Higher Education
Research Reports

This index provides immediate access to the subject content of the
10 monographs in the 1983 ASHE-ERIC Higher Education Research Report series. Entries are followed by a Report number in
bold type as well as page numbers listed in chronological se-
quence. Entries with only Report numbers indicate that the
subject heading is the main focus of that Report.

E

Educational excellence (*see* Academic standards)
Employment
> burnout in, **9**
> practices, **2; 8**
Equal pay, **8**:9, 45-65
Evaluation (*see also* Peer review; Program evaluation; Self-regulation)
> reports, utilization of, **1**:55, 56

F

Faculty
> applicants, **2**:31-38
> burnout, **9**
> career paths, **3**:2, 3,17-32; **9**:37-47
> competence, **6**:80-86
> contract termination, **2**:13-15
> coping with stress, **9**:54-75
> disability or death, **2**:16
> employment issues, **8**
> goal congruence and loyalty, **10**:36, 37
> impact of technology, **3**:36, 37
> in distance education, **5**:9-15
> involuntary separation, **2**:9-11
> mandatory retirement, **8**:81-107
> new, **2**:45-54
> nonrenewal, **8**:20-44
> orientation, **2**:48-51
> performance of, **1**:50, 51
> power, **10**:32-35
> promotion, **2**:11-13; **8**:20-44
> psychological outcomes, **3**:24-26
> recruitment, **2**:24-44
> retention, **2**:45-56
> reward structure, **3**:34-36; **5**:10; **7**:103-107
> role in learning improvement, **4**:60-65
> salary, **2**:17-20; **8**:9, 45-65, 104, 105
> termination of tenured, **8**:91, 92
> vacancies, **2**:6-16, 24-29
> work environment, **9**:30-53
> work experience, **10**:16-44

Faculty development, **2**:52-54; **3**:3, 27-32
Federal aid, **1**:10-12
Federal regulation, **1**:10-14

Orientation
>distance education, **5**:37, 38
>new faculty, **2**:48-51

P

Paraprofessional staff, **4**:60-65

Partnerships (*see* Cooperative arrangements)

Peer review, **8**:30-34

Personality and stress, **9**:18-53

Personnel (*see* Administrators, Employment, Faculty, Support Staff)

Personnel policy, **2**; **3**
>employee development, **10**:70-72, 91
>organizational structure, **10**:11-14, 66-72

Planning
>distance education, **5**:43, 44
>faculty recruitment, **2**:17-23

Policymaking, developmental programs, **4**:51-60

Presidents, work experience, **10**:45-53, 80, 81

Professional staff, **4**:60-65

Program development, **4**:20-75

Program evaluation
>academic quality, **1**:34-55
>distance education, difficulty in, **5**:47, 48
>learning improvement, **4**:66-75

Public service
>as a mission, **7**:9-27
>exemplary approaches to, **7**:65-71
>organizing for, **7**:95-110
>recommendations for, **7**:111-114
>resources for, **7**:107-110
>to business and industry, **7**:72-94
>to community, **7**:28-53
>to government, **7**:54-71

Q

Quality assurance, **1**

R

Registration, in distance education, **5**:38

Remedial programs, **4**

Research
>academic workplace, agenda for, **10**:72-74
>administrator work experience, summary and direction, **10**:82-84, 88-90

U

Urban institutions, **7**:49-53

V

Video technology in instruction, **5**:16-24

W

Work environment, **2**:45-47; **9**:30-53; **10**:11-15
Work experience
        administrators, **10**:45-65, 82-84, 88-90
        deans and department chairs, **10**:62-65
        faculty, **10**:16-44, 76-79, 85-87
        presidents, **10**:45-53, 80, 81
        support and clerical staff, **10**:91

AUTHOR INDEX
1983 ASHE-ERIC Higher Education Research Reports

This index lists the authors and their report numbers for the 10 monographs in the 1983 Higher Eudcation Research Report Series.